west marin review

SUMMER 2009

02

A Publishing Collaboration

TOMALES BAY LIBRARY ASSOCIATION
POINT REYES BOOKS
NEIGHBORS & FRIENDS

VOLUME II • SUMMER 2009

PROSE

POETRY

ART + ARTIFACT

OPPOSITE C.R. Snyder, *Election Sign on the Grandi Building*, 2007

coffee @
Toby's

Dear Reader

WELCOME to the *West Marin Review*, a community partnership and 99 percent volunteer effort featuring both fine and homespun art, prose, and poetry. This year's theme is "Who We Are, Where We Come From." Without our trying to make it so, the works in the first volume and this second one share an appreciation for the natural world, an attention to the details of life and the vastness of it, and honest perspectives on subjects from agrarian to urbane.

There is an editorial hand, of course. Most content is selected by "reviewers": a panel for poetry, one for prose, and a team of artists reviewing art. Submissions (for this volume there were approximately 450) are reviewed without panel members knowing the identity of writers or artists. Some pieces, like the Tomales High contributions, were solicited. Content this year was chosen for how relative it was to our fairly elastic theme.

The theme causes background to become foreground in this volume, with family figuring prominently in many of our writers' memories and imaginations: the haunting short stories feature a brother and sister in Elizabeth Leahy's "whitebird"

Igor Sazevich, *Point Reyes Morning Spaces*, 2008, pen-and-ink drawing, 7 1/2 x 5 inches and a mother and son in Rosaleen Bertolino's "Silverton." Philip Fradkin remembers his mother here. There are childhoods revisited in a slice of cherry pie, in song and dance, in a ball made of lead gum wrappers. There is life revisited: Joanne Kyger talks with Steve Heilig about her poetry and past.

Our contributors, residents and visitors to West Marin, are from everywhere—East Coast, West Coast, South of the Border, overseas—and they are every sort of people: in addition to professional writers, artists, and poets, there are psychotherapists, teachers, students, innkeepers, house cleaners, carpenters, and at least one attorney and one firefighter that we know of.

And as in Volume One of the *Review,* in which "The Geography of Hope" was the theme, place is no less important in Volume Two. Blair Fuller provides a charming stereoptic history of the town of Tomales and himself along with it. Annet Held's photographs from the 1950s document a Dutch world she came from that doesn't exist any more. The Tomales High Mural Project and the Marin Literacy Photography Project put different lenses on the place we know as West Marin, as John Anderson's painting does on molecular, energetic, and cosmic space.

In this issue, poetry, prose, and art are direct and oblique, whimsical and serious, inward observing and outward observing. You'll find history in a story here, in a mural, in yellowed cross-written letters preserved by a family; you'll see art in a poet's handwritten poem, in the serendipity of pinhole photographs; and you'll glimpse evidence of the poets' and the artists' way of seeing, microscopically and magnificently.

POEM Joanne Kyger, *About Now* (excerpt), 2003
ART Art One Students, Tomales High School, *Black Mountain, Point Reyes National Seashore,* 2008, pinhole Holga photograph

Home is the moment
the quail arrive

Amanda Tomlin, *Winter Night,* 2007, silver gelatin print, 8 x 10 inches

The Birds and the Beef

Laurel Wroten

HOW MANY naïve West Marin newcomers, blind to the fickle ways of both Mother Nature and the local utility grid, have been lured by the siren call of freezer meat? Quite a few, I've discovered, though my particular story is perhaps more unusual than most. The plot may be strange, but its moral is simple: if you've got half a cow in your deep freeze, make sure you've also got a functioning generator.

Back in the fall of '01, my husband and I had barely unpacked our moving boxes when the opportunity to buy our meat "on the hoof" first presented itself. The term "on the hoof," for you greenhorns who still shop retail, translates roughly to "Congratulations! You've got enough inventory to open a butcher shop!" Remember the famous question, "Where's the beef?" I can provide the answer. It's in my freezer, along with the pig, the lamb, the hindquarter of a goat, and a couple of good-sized chickens. Any day now, they'll be joined by a side of mutton.

You'd think I'd have learned my lesson after all that has transpired, but I am a freezer-meat recidivist. If one of my ranching neighbors wants to sell me half a steer, say, or a quarter-interest in a Berkshire hog, I am as helpless as a vintage-toy addict with a high-speed Internet hook-up to eBay. Some women have a weakness for shoes; I satisfy my inner Imelda Marcos by purchasing meat in bulk. The way I figure it, why simply pick up a couple of steaks at retail when I can, for just a house payment or two more, have an entire frozen barnyard in my basement? It is, I'm forced to admit, the closest I'll ever come to having a farm of my own.

As a person who can barely cope with the occasional errant mouse, let alone anything that could reasonably qualify as a 4-H project, I nonetheless long to fit into this community of hardy, self-reliant people. Buying my meat directly from a local rancher, besides being extremely virtuous from an ecological point of view, also makes me feel like an active participant in the local agricultural scene. Farmers and ranchers are the Brahmins of West Marin society, if only because the rest of us stand in awe of people who can string barbed wire with their bare hands and who also possess a vast storehouse of information on esoteric subjects we know absolutely nothing about, like crop yield ratios and the most reliable brands of automatic-milking machines. When I drop by Toby's or the post office, I like to run into ranching folk I've done a little business with, especially if I'm in the company of visitors from over the hill, who are invariably impressed with my connections. Though since acquiring all this meat, I don't really have time for visitors; I'm too busy rendering lard and making my own head cheese.

A freezer full of animal parts does pose its share of creative challenges. West Marin is crawling with talented artistic types: painters, photographers, poets, sculptors, novelists, filmmakers, and so on, and I am proud to count myself among them. My own particular medium happens to be obscure cuts of meat. When you buy on the hoof, you receive, in addition to the steaks and chops and other things that are normally classified as food, a fair amount of what butchers sometimes refer to as "variety cuts," those odds and ends of mystery meat that in saner circumstances are typically sold under the Alpo label. Transforming a lamb's brain or the lining of a pig's intestine into something a Homo sapiens might even begin to approach with a fork may not be on a par with plein-air landscape painting, but it has its own quiet rewards.

Unfortunately, my hobby also has a serious downside, which first became apparent in the early winter of 2002, when a massive

Pacific storm slammed into the Point Reyes area, bringing two straight days of gale-force winds and enough rain to turn parts of the region into a kind of Venice with cows.

At the time, my husband and I had only been living out here for a few months and we were thrilled to be caught up in this significant meteorological event—until the moment we realized that the pump carrying water from our storage tank to the house required a flow of electricity to work. Whatever romantic illusions I might have been harboring about rural living quickly vanished when we started hauling in buckets of rainwater to flush the toilet. Beyond our occasional run-ins with the spa heater, our previous incarnation as Mill Valley suburbanites had left us ill prepared for much in the way of domestic adversity.

Nonetheless, we were getting a handle on things! We had one flashlight and at least three D batteries whose use-by dates hadn't expired, along with some floating candles left over from the previous summer, and we were making a valiant effort to get into the indoor camping spirit. We were even thinking it might be fun to roast up a few s'mores in the fireplace, which so far was only smoking a little. We'd just cracked open a nice bottle of pinot noir and were feeling pretty good about our new life in the wilderness when we remembered the three hundred pounds of meat stacked up in the freezer downstairs.

By the time Day Six arrived and it was clear that PG&E was not going to rescue us any time soon, we began to contemplate our options. The meat was surely thawed by this time, though we hadn't yet worked up the courage to check, but there was no chance of getting through more than a roast or two before the unwelcome visitors would begin to arrive: *escherichia coli* and *salmonella profundi,* for starters, followed in quick succession by *clostridium perfringens, staphylococcus aureus,* and *campylobacter jejuni*—all Latin, of course, for "better pick up a case of Kaopectate." We toyed briefly with the idea of inviting all the neighbors in for a huge barbecue, but our grill was small and the weather soggy, and we figured no one would come anyway. People who have been without power for nearly a week, particularly those with electric septic pumps, are generally not in the most festive of moods. So we moved on to Plan B.

Turkey vultures can be extremely useful birds. Unlike hawks, who must hunt for their meals, TVs—as many birders call them—dine exclusively on creatures that somebody else, quite often an inattentive driver, has dispatched. We'd noticed there were often a fair number of these large, mopey-looking birds in the vicinity of our house, probably due to the succession of hairpin turns on the stretch of highway leading up to our driveway. A shortage of road kill, sad to say, is not generally a problem around our place.

With their bald red heads and hunched-up shoulders, the vultures were undeniably homely, but we'd taken a liking to them anyway. Their unsavory dietary habits, it turned out, had a bright side: every time I saw a dead animal by the roadside I felt a little better knowing that fortune at least had smiled on some nearby turkey vulture, who would now have a nice meal to bring home to his family. Sometimes, when the carnage was particularly depressing, I tried to visualize baby turkey vultures snuggled into their nest, eagerly anticipating their next meal of regurgitated venison. The Holy Spirit is traditionally represented as a dove, perhaps a more conventionally attractive bird, but these vultures, despite their unsightly appearance, served as a tangible reminder of cosmic truth: that out of death springs life—a pretty impressive feat, when you think about it, for a creature that keeps cool by defecating on its own legs.

Since the storm had begun, the TVs were looking particularly glum, slumped in a bedraggled row on the nonfunctioning power lines and trying without much success to air out their sodden wings. They had the attitude, I thought, of undertakers on a break. And they were probably hungry. Because of the flooding, no traffic had gotten through our section of highway in days. But their luck was about to change.

Though my husband's carpentry skills are somewhat limited, he set about constructing a backyard feeding platform from the odds and ends of scrap lumber that seem to come standard with every house around here. It was a matter of utmost importance that the platform be elevated to a level beyond the reach of our two standard poodles. These dogs have extremely delicate digestive systems and are restricted to a diet of bland prescription kibble even the resident raccoons refuse to steal. The potential consequences of allowing our pets unfettered access to thawed-out freezer meat were much too terrifying to contemplate.

By Day Seven, the weather had cleared a bit, and our vulture feeder was ready for action. We headed down to the basement, held our breaths, and gingerly cracked open the freezer lid. Much to our relief, we were not blown over by the stench of rotten meat or an avalanche of writhing maggots. Everything was thawed out and a little waterlogged, but still cool to the touch. We had no idea if the vultures would even be attracted to meat that still smelled okay and was not attached to a carcass, so we decided to start small. We pulled out a grass-fed tri-tip, a pork tenderloin, and a one-pound package of hamburger. Then we headed out to the back field, tossed the meat up onto the feeding platform, and returned to the house to wait with our binoculars.

I can confirm that even the most sophisticated surveillance equipment in our government's military arsenal has nothing on the Vulture Meat Detection System. We were barely back indoors when our first potential customer appeared. He was little more than a black dot in the sky to begin with, but he proceeded to zero in quickly on the feeder, tilting himself one way and then the other as he circled overhead, clearly on a reconnaissance mission. Soon a dozen or so other TVs drifted over to join him, and it wasn't long before the birds decided in near unison to land on the roof of our shed, a convenient resting spot that provided them an excellent view of our little smorgasbord while they tried to figure out what to do next. They looked more cheerful already. After about fifteen minutes of what appeared to be a lot of muttering back and forth, one bird suddenly made his move and flew over to the feeding platform, where he eyed the selection briefly and then ripped off a hunk of tri-tip. The party was officially on.

Over the next several days, the menu at our TV Diner included rack of lamb, beef heart, top round, porterhouse steaks, chuck roast, oxtail, and pig's trotters. Word had gotten out in the larger turkey vulture community, and we suspected that birds from as far away as Sebastopol and Rohnert Park were now coming by to check things out. These were giddy times in the TV world. For creatures accustomed to a steady diet of flattened skunk and moldering possum, it was like going from the mess hall at San Quentin to the downstairs dining room of Chez Panisse. Things were a little crazy. Managing the skies above our house would have been a challenge for even the most seasoned air traffic controller. There were vultures flying through the air with pot roasts in their talons, vultures clutching pork chops in their bills, and vultures so stuffed they could barely gain altitude.

By the time power was restored, around Day Eleven, we had managed to give away about half our meat stash. We decided that the sensible thing, given our mounting concerns about sanitation, would be to refreeze the remaining portion and thaw a few packages at a time to feed to the vultures. And so the backyard bacchanal continued, until the inevitable day when we reached the end of our supply.

A disappointed turkey vulture is a sorry sight to behold. Seventy-five disappointed turkey vultures, on the other hand, is a ready-made cast for the remake of a Hitchcock movie. The birds were everywhere, waiting in eerie silence. (Unlike other birds, TVs are strangely mute, anatomically incapable of all but a modest repertoire of hisses and grunts.) Some of them stood on the feeding platform, some perched in nearby trees, and one large group had begun assembling on the roof of our house. Others hovered outside our windows, trying to peer in. Birds dive-bombed us when we stepped out to get the morning paper or when we tried to run the gauntlet from the front porch to the spot where we'd parked our truck, a vehicle that was now in dire need of a trip to the carwash. Call me crazy, but I began to think that the TVs were also starting to show an unusual interest in the dogs.

We decided that cutting the vultures off cold turkey, so to speak, had probably been unwise. Despite the financial hit we'd already taken as a result of the freezer meltdown, which we calculated at $1018.63, or exactly $18.63 above the deductible on our homeowners' policy, we agreed that our most prudent course would be to start buying the birds meat. We hoped that they wouldn't object to dining on specially reduced closeouts from Costco, a definite step down from the eight-dollar-a-pound, pasture-raised and organically certified offerings they had come to expect. But there were limits to our largesse. I waited until the vultures had tucked in for the night, then made a dash for the truck and headed to Santa Rosa.

Slowly, we managed to wean them. First we skipped one day, then two, then three, and pretty soon we were down to feeding the birds just once a week. By the time six weeks had passed, we'd stopped buying meat for them altogether. Every so often, I would toss out the occasional chicken gizzard or maybe some pork that had gone slimy in the fridge, but beyond that, the vultures' meal ticket was once again in the hands of Mother Nature and the always-reliable supply of crazy drivers and suicidal deer. Our avian visitors gradually returned to their former routine, idly cruising by every now and then in hopes of an unexpected windfall, but they seemed more or less resigned to the fact that their holiday from roadside scrounging had come to an end. Life at our place was at last returning to normal. We bought a fancy new generator, specially programmed to kick on automatically whenever there was a voltage reduction in the PG&E lines—extra security in case we were away—and we put in a second propane tank for the generator to run on. Then I started stocking up on freezer meat again.

When the next huge storm hit, in the winter of '04, my husband and I were sitting on the beach in Key Biscayne, Florida, drinking banana daiquiris and deeply engrossed in the plots of our respective paperbacks, the sort of cheesy potboilers that are widely sold at airports but rarely occupy shelf space around Point Reyes. But, guess what, we were on vacation! We could wave at Republicans (using all four fingers) and gorge on greasy snacks made with GMO corn and a long list of unpronounceable ingredients, and we could read novels of absolutely no redeeming social value! Best of all, we could appear in public without wearing fleece, which we'd been brazenly doing for four days now, possibly an all-time record. The temperature was a pleasant 84 degrees, the wind was balmy, and needless to say, our freezer was not foremost in our minds.

But several days later, when we pulled into our driveway around 11 p.m., groggy with jet lag and in mild shock from the change in climate, it was immediately obvious that things were not as they should be. For starters, everything was pitch black, despite the fact that the porch lights had been on when we left. When we opened the car doors, we were greeted by the unmistakable drone of our neighbor's ancient generator. Our new, state-of-the-art model, the one with all the bells and whistles, seemed to be strangely silent.

Exhausted, we decided that further investigation would have to wait until morning. We dragged our bags up the dark front porch steps and entered the cold and silent house, the house with no running water or working toilets, the house with the freezer full of meat in the basement—meat that appeared, once again, to have a rendezvous with destiny.

When the next day dawned, we discovered that the earthquake shut-off valve on the propane line leading into our new generator had been tripped—by what, or whom we'll never know. According to the

Rich Clarke, *Martinelli Bull, Highway One,* 2006

neighbors, there hadn't been an earthquake during our absence, even a tiny one. In any event, we knew what we had to do. That afternoon, we put up the feeder and got out our binoculars, scanning the skies as our old scavenger friends returned to their favorite dining spot. They seemed excited—for vultures, anyway, probably feeling a bit like swallows do on their first day back in Capistrano. It might have been my imagination playing tricks, but a couple of them looked a little guilty as well.

Nancy Stein, *Wave #44*, 2007, pastel on paper, 15 x 24 inches

Finding Beauty in a Broken World

Terry Tempest Williams

We watched the towers collapse. We watched America choose war.
The peace in our own hearts shattered.

How to pick up the pieces?
What to do with these pieces?

I was desperate to retrieve the poetry I had lost.

Standing on a rocky point in Maine, looking east toward the horizon at dusk, I faced the ocean. *"Give me one wild word."* It was all I asked of the sea.

The tide was out. The mudflats exposed. A gull picked up a large white clam, hovered high above the rocks, then dropped it. The clam broke open, and the gull swooped down to eat the fleshy animal inside.

"Give me one wild word to follow..."

And the word the sea rolled back to me was "m o s a i c."

Late September Song

Linda Pastan

With the sound of
a freight train
rushing
through the trees,
the first strong
wind

of autumn
makes each
leaf
sing the song
of its own
execution.

Elise Kroeber, *Marsh at Bodega*, 1980

Gale S. McKee, *On The Road,* 2007, acrylic on canvas, 36 x 30 inches

whitebird

Elizabeth Leahy

THE WIND had come up like it did every afternoon from across the bay, but stronger always moving into November, so that there in my old shake-shingle place up on the bluff, the lighting of a fire at the stone hearth had something to do with timing. He was more patient than I remembered, until a great gust rattled the thick glass of the front windows, lifted my brother to his feet, and sent him flying out the door, running downhill with his boots unlaced and his shirttails flapping. It froze my heart to hear the door slam and turn from the stove to see him gone, but when I went to look after him, when he started cutting left then right to slow down his approach to the coast road, it was then that I saw what my brother had seen. Something white. Maybe six feet wide. Feathered at either end. Caught on the top line of barbed wire just above a wooden rail. Legs or tail dangling. The whole thing pinned and whipped by the wind.

What I knew made me turn away from the front door and wait, holding back one desperate hound dog all bucking and whining and twisting my hand around inside his collar. What I knew, I had time to doubt while I waited, sitting on the arm of the couch at the far end of the front room when the door opened and he entered, out of breath, a quick smile then shaking his head like he was tricked again, fell for it again, as he reached inside his shirt and pulled out a large white plastic bag.

I was the only real family he had out here and he was that for me; he had come for the first time in three years and there we sat, forks pushing around fried potatoes and fish, the hound lying under the table with his head on my brother's foot; something unexpected coming around to remind you who you are and where you've been.

He had wanted to turn back just twenty miles outside of town, heading south and getting close to the ramp for the I-15 towards Idaho Falls. He had jammed on the brakes and pounded the steering wheel and cursed my name when he saw me in the rearview mirror clawing at the window, no longer able to hold on to the tie-down hooks in the back of the rusted-out pickup with rotted layers of plywood and nails where the bed should have been. Where I had quietly placed myself after following him unnoticed for three days, seeing him doing things he never did, seeing how he was preparing for something, and fearful that all of it added up to his leaving. Then on the very day, I had come so close to missing him, tossing and waking and sleeping in bits and pieces. But I listened, and waited. And when he woke I let him go out before I moved and, last minute, thought to grab a crusted wool blanket from the shed where our old-girl hound had her pups. I kept safe enough behind him crossing town so that when he opened the truck door, quietly slipped into neutral and out the open bay of my uncle's body shop around 3 a.m. on a Sunday, end of August, I felt somehow that if I stayed low and timed my boarding with the cough and growl of the engine, I might have a chance.

So there we were in a stolen truck. Me praying. Him cursing. But after a time, nodding towards me to come around front, and reaching across to lift the door lock; maybe in a moment of relief that his plan to disappear from Butte undetected had not really been ruined, so long as he carried his younger sister away with him, his only witness.

Idaho turned into Utah and dawn came as a red line on the horizon, but it wasn't until we had almost reached Salt Lake City that the rain started down. We could have been driving for days, for how hungry I felt. For how uncertain I felt, folding and refolding a torn map that ended at Reno. Still there was no navigating through the hours of thinking maybe the hardness of what you left was better than the worry of not knowing what was ahead; or through the strange desolation of Nevada where after miles of nothing but sagebrush there would appear a long cinderblock building with three flashing signs: Live-Nude-Girls! next to Liquor-Cigarettes-Deli next to Live-Bait-Nightcrawlers (and not a drop of water in sight)—something to help us both laugh, and talk a minute about what the ocean would be like when we finally got to California—before we'd fall back again, for the longest time, to the quiet. Because there in the air between us, in the musty smell of the upholstery, in the red dust that clung to the small lines of our hands and to the stitches of our boots was this: We'd both had enough.

It had snowed all night long and our father woke up with a bad back and a bad headache so instead of my brother and him going to pick up some track belt for the plow it was me pushed awake before dawn to help do the digging or freezing alongside the road if we happened to get stuck. Those days, always wiseass and mad, my brother decided to take the shortcut across the old mine road, which I knew for sure was a bad idea for its winding steepness as you got near the ridge. There you could see how the pit getting bigger made more homes disappear: ranches and gardens and hillsides and trees; coyotes, gophers, snakes, birds, gone. And when there was no more copper to be found, after the smaller tunnel mines pumping the heavy acid water out of their own way had shut down, the red-brown liquid flowed over to fill the pit, so that now, in the dim light of a November morning, with that white blanket around its edges and a foggy mist rising from its middle, you might think you had just naturally come upon a sleeping lake. Which is what must have happened to the Snow Geese that night.

Stop jamming the brakes, I said. Like you know how to drive? he said. Slipping and fish-tailing for a mile downhill, so focused on holding the road, maybe we were balanced on the edge of fear and disbelief, for the closer we got to level, the more it seemed like the top of the lake was boiling. Then unreal turned to awful. There must have been hundreds of them, tired from their journey, needing to stop for a bit of a rest. Some already washed ashore. Some still floating. So many more still landing and flapping, up and down and trying again, as if they could not open their eyes to the ruin.

When my brother pulled over to the edge of the pit, I did not ask why and he did not say come on. I opened my door and he opened his door and soon we were thigh-high in ice water, pulling Snow Geese from a poison lake.

Close to noon many more people had come—people we knew from town or church or school—everyone saying, you kids go home now, you done what you could. Offering us a blanket or a thermos. No heat in the truck would make for one long ride, and longer still if we kept driving to get that part for the plow, so we did like they said and headed home. How a tired man with a bad back could swing a bat so hard I do not know. But my brother had been inside the door not one minute to get us some dry clothes when I saw his arm go up and his head go down, and then the big stick, which had come at him from behind, as if the old man was waiting; had already decided to strike.

After Reno, just before the state line, things finally started looking up. God, that crystal clear lake. The granite peaks. High mountain air and perfect sky. I was wide-eyed, without a penny, and could not stop smiling. We laughed so much. We talked about what kind of work we might find. We made promises. We said the words: I hope.

Earthly Catalogue

Nell Sullivan

Before all goes velvet in my eyes, I need to see where I've been.
I need to know what there was when
I saw the color of the sunset shadows over the hills,
green convex, gray concave go all purple/rosy, how willow leaf green.

It's not in fashion to say, I'm going blind.
Any more than to say, god damn it,
your cat's pissed my pillow again. It stinks.
Nothing to do about either one.

The color vanishes.
The stench prevails.

No washing removes the ineffable whiff in the corner
of my favorite dream.
No refraction cures the inevitability of grayness
of fading sharp cut gravel heaped in geometric shapes over the green
convex, gray concave, all purple rosy, willow leaf green sloping hills,
the rolling catalogue of the before.

Happy Mistakes

Pinhole Photography by Art One Students
Rachel Somerville, Teacher

TOMALES HIGH SCHOOL

STUDENTS OFTEN struggle with a concern for perfection and a preconception that "good art" should be a precise rendition of real life. For a lesson in accepting the power of chance and happenstance in creative work, Art One students at Tomales High School received pinhole Holga cameras and were assigned to photograph the landscapes in which they live.

The pinhole camera is unpredictable because of its simplicity. There are no viewfinders, digital screens, or zoom lenses. The shutter, a flap of some light-proof material, is usually manually operated, covering and uncovering a pinhole cut into one side of a light-proof box. The smaller the hole, the sharper the image. Though the photographer has little control, resulting images are full of unexpected, beautiful mistakes.

OPPOSITE AND ABOVE Art One Students, Tomales High School, *Two Views of Papermill Creek, On the Road Towards Inverness,* 2008, pinhole Holga photograph

Art One Students, Tomales High School,
Black Mountain, Point Reyes National Seashore,
2008, pinhole Holga photographs

Art One Students, Tomales High School,
Tomales High School Football Field, 2008,
pinhole Holga photographs

JENNY HAIKU

I WATCHED MY CAT'S TAIL
TWITCH LIKE AN EMERGING WORM
AFTER THE FIRST RAIN

—Jon Langdon, *Jenny Haiku*

If We Should Die Tomorrow

Eugenia Loyster

Crenelating the beached
humpback whale, long dead,
were peaks of birds
transforming whale into
vulture, gull, raven.

Alan said, "I'd like
to go that way,
unresisting on the shore
slowly being changed,
growing wings."

The women thought they
preferred being food for
roses; Millay had been
the poet of their youth.

Hiding Out with Joanne Kyger, Poet of West Marin

Steve Heilig

"The knowledge of the 1000-year sigh in Joanne Kyger's genius!"
—Ed Sanders, "Ode to the Beat Generation," 2008

Night Palace

'The best thing about the past
is that it's over'
when you die.
you wake up
from the dream
that's your life.
Then you grow up
and get to be post human
in a past that keeps happening
ahead of you

October 2003

MODERN POETRY is for many readers something like the emperor's new clothes. Although we are supposed to "see" and appreciate it, few of us do. The abstraction, the willful difficulty and obscure references prevalent in much "good" poetry are like medicine we suspect must be good for us simply because it tastes bad. So while many people profess to like it, few regularly read good poetry. Thus it's all the more rewarding to find that rare poet whose words are neither a clever labyrinth of abstraction nor simplistic pap, but something that allows us to see things from new angles—and even to laugh while doing so.

John Anderson, *SIME,* 1980, acrylic on canvas, 72 x 36 inches

Joanne Kyger, who is one such poet, may be widely renowned for her writing, but she's not that easy to find. She is a longtime denizen of a Marin coastal village with no road signs leading to it—or rather, with many such signs, all of which are safely hidden in residents' homes and garages. She has never courted wider renown than that which comes to her naturally. But come to her it has, at least among those who love a creative use of words, of lines and space on the page, and of imagery and feeling.

Kyger was born in Vallejo in 1934; her father was a career Navy officer whose travels took his family to China and then Southern California, where Kyger grew up. She studied at the University of California in Santa Barbara and then found herself, at the age of 23, in San Francisco's North Beach just when Allen Ginsberg's publisher, Lawrence Ferlinghetti, was on trial for obscenity for publishing Ginsberg's legendary poem, "Howl." Already beginning to write poetry of her own, Kyger found the late-1950s ferment there encouraging and was soon associated with the fabled "Beat" writing milieu. She studied with or at least knew many of the leading literary figures of that time and place, including Robert Duncan, Jack Spicer, Jack Kerouac, Ginsberg, Philip Whalen, Richard Brautigan, Lew Welch, and Gary Snyder—writers whose works remain popular and collected around the world. She was one of only a few female writers of this iconoclastic and fabled cadre to gain respect on her own terms, both among peers and readers.

Kyger's first book of poems, *The Tapestry and the Web,* was published in 1965. After extended travels to Asia with Ginsberg and Snyder (to whom she was married at the time), Kyger settled in West Marin in 1969, buying a house that committed her to a tiny monthly mortgage. "I didn't always have a lot left over to be able to leave town, so I stayed out here a lot," she recalls.

Since then Kyger has published steadily, if not especially prolifically, with twenty mostly brief collections of poems, journals, and other writings appearing over the past three decades. But a relative flurry of printed collections of her work has appeared in more recent years, including *Again: Poems 1989–2000; Some Life;* and a reprint of *Strange Big Moon: Japan and India Journals, 1960–1964.* In recognition of her cumulative body of work, *As Ever,* a selection culled from her lifetime of poetry to date, appeared in 2002 as part of the prestigious Penguin Poets series. In 2007 the National Poetry Foundation brought out *About Now: Collected Poems*—a nearly 800-page "doorstop" (her term), featuring more than 400 poems published from 1957 to 2004. She has also traveled somewhat more extensively than in those early years, especially to Mexico; and she teaches, gives readings, and lectures around the country and in Europe.

But Kyger is still most comfortable in her original West Marin home, sharing it with her longtime partner, fellow writer and illustrator Donald Guravich. Their house and garden are, appropriately enough, hidden behind a huge hedge off a dirt road. But as a voracious reader and viewer of the events of the broader world, Kyger remains notably informed and concerned about goings-on "over the hill," and for years has infused not only her writing but also a weekly version of the local village paper, which she often edits, with political commentary and satire from many sources.

As for her primary work, poetry, she is often reluctant to speak of it. Others, though, praise it unreservedly. The late Robert Creeley, one of the most revered poets of the past half century, said, "There is no poet with more whimsically tough a mind.... She's the best of the West." Nobel Prize-winning author Czeslaw Milosz, in compiling his 1996 international poetry anthology, *A Book of Luminous Things,* chose not just one of her poems as he did for the other notable contributors to the volume, but two. Allen Ginsberg took her portrait for one of her books; Richard Brautigan dedicated one of his own best-loved novellas, *In Watermelon Sugar,* to her; and fellow poet David Meltzer, in his introduction to a collection of her poems, declared, "No other poet of my generation has been able to make the pleasures and particulars of the 'everyday' as luminous and essential and central." And in one of the early reviews of her work, the reviewer wrote, "Let us propose that Joanne Kyger is a genius, though a weird one."

The object of all this acclaim is herself a tall, elegant, self-effacing woman with a twinkle in her eyes—usually partially concealed behind tinted glasses—who obviously loves words and will talk enthusiastically and/or caustically about nearly anything, other than herself (Creeley also noted that she has "an almost confusing demur in respect to prizes or any such games poets play"). But here is some of what she said in a recent interview about her own life and work, and about life in West Marin and beyond.

Your book of selected poems, As Ever, *was dedicated "To Those who love to read." Do you remember your own first loves in this regard—what did you most love to read?*

As a child in the early 1940s, I was living in a small town in Illinois, and of course there wasn't any television yet, and so reading was something you could do for sheer escapism, the ability to be transported somewhere else. So I read constantly, even before I could really understand what I was reading. I'd just skip over words and parts I didn't "get"—maybe that's why I ended up such a bad speller. And it was portable, you could take a book anywhere with you. So I read all the *Wizard of Oz* books, *Dr. Doolittle,* the *Nancy Drew* novels, and lots of magical adventures with caves and princesses and such.

When did you first realize you would become a writer yourself?

In my small school, they had us memorizing poetry a lot. Lots of Longfellow, and I think the first poet I was really struck by was Robert Service, "The Creation of Sam McGee." I thought that was just as thrilling as you could get.

I don't think many kids have to memorize such things anymore.

Probably not, but I'm really glad I did. A whole classroom would recite it out loud. Maybe they do rap songs now. There's the iambic pentameter rhythm that make the words accessible to memory.

Do you recall what you were trying to "do" with your first attempts at writing?

I think I thought about amusing people, entertaining them. So at ten or twelve years old, I did class assignments, writing poetry monologues. And in high school I wrote features for the school paper. And by college I had read and heard—on records—T. S. Eliot, Dylan Thomas, and especially William Carlos Williams.

After college in Santa Barbara, you came to San Francisco. Was it the Beat poetry scene that drew you there?

No, I wasn't even really aware of it yet. But then there was the Ginsberg "Howl" trial, and I started going to poetry and jazz performances, and there was excitement, electricity in the air. I was writing all the time and somebody invited me to a writing group led by Robert Duncan and Jack Spicer, and after a few meetings they said I would have to read out loud, too. It went over OK. So essentially that became my "path," as it were, as I could see that people like Ginsberg and Gary Snyder were major identities, and that you could say you were a poet and through that identity be interested in virtually anything. And also, at that time it was about "How do you stop feeling so screwed up, and get over your neuroses?" Everyone seemed to feel that through Buddhism or psychoanalysis or understanding your dreams you could do better and maybe be less intense, which was one of my problems.

So eventually I joined Gary in Japan to "do" Zen, and I kept writing and some got published and then after I returned in 1964, my first book was published the next year.

How has living in West Marin over the decades influenced your writing?

I moved out here in 1968. There was that big back-to-the-land movement then, and a few writers had already figured out that you could survive. John and Margot Doss had a house here and she was very generous about letting writers stay there to get their bearings, and supportive of publisher Don Allen, who had the Four Seasons press here (later Grey Fox), who published a lot of us early on, such as Philip Whalen. And there were a fair number of other local presses started here as well, like Angel Hair, Coyote, Big Sky, Smithereens, and Tombuctou. And in the early 1970s Tom Clark here was poetry editor of the *Paris Review,* a big deal, and published his friends.

It's really amazing what a literary presence this area was, considering what a small community it is—people even refer to it as a distinct "school" of poetry.

Yes. And it was quite an era, really. Most of us were in our 20s and 30s and it was a time when we were figuring out how to do our art, have households and babies, and sort out what it was all about. The environmental movement was getting underway and it was a real "greening out" in this area. There was a strong sense of communal living, and of being "organic," whatever that meant then. It was possible to get by on very little.

And this affected the writing going on here too?

Yes, the whole frame of reference shifted, to the landscape and the weather, the place, which we all had in common. There was always this natural magic going on, and the news was just right outside your window. And it was a small-town feeling—you could spend all day getting somebody's old truck out of the mud, and it was a big adventure. And then there'd be a bunch of poems about it.

When did you see this era coming to an end?

That came in the '80s. It became less bucolic, and people drifted away, usually for real reasons, such as having to make a living, children going to different schools. There was a certain wild openness here, which lessened as a more cultivated gardening approach came in. But again, the human community is also part of the attraction of being in a place like this.

Back to the writing itself: What was revolutionary about the San Francisco Renaissance? Your first publisher, Don Allen, described it as having "a new attitude toward mind, nature, and society...of the primordial, of spiritual and sexual necessities." But he also called it "postmodernism."

Hmm. I'm still trying to figure out what "modernism" is or was, let alone postmodern.

My favorite cultural critic, Homer Simpson, called postmodernism something that is "complicated for the sake of being complicated."

That sounds about right. But that's certainly not me, I hope. For myself, I thought about the other Homer, the old Greek who wrote about great journeys and stories of life, and the multiplicity of gods and goddesses, and omens and signs. After a while your poetry fits your landscape, or it should if you want to be literally grounded and interesting. Otherwise you're just writing in your head, and let's face it, most heads aren't all that different or interesting in themselves. It's language talking about language. Poetry should say what's going on. The established, East Coast schools of poetry had become very dry, academic, abstract, and out West the writing was a reaction to that.

Your friend and fellow poet, Lew Welch, who also lived in Marin, said he wanted to have his poetry understood by people down in the bar, not just in the university.

And I, too, wanted to make my writing accessible. I even once wrote a poem about making it so accessible that it would be like baby talk. Really, it's about trying to find a common language.

You've also said that poems are best read aloud. Do you write with that in mind? You are particular about how your poems are laid out on the page.

Yes. You want to make it so that someone could say it. I try to "score" the lines for the page with that in mind, the breathing, the timing.

You've mentioned Buddhism, and many of your fellow poets are identified with that, particularly Zen. Does that affect your writing?

Buddhism can make you aware of the interconnectedness of things, and is sophisticated about how the mind works, which is helpful for a writer. I do meditate, but it's a little tussle to do it every day. But again, when you think about Marin, I've been fortunate to be kind of entranced and informed by the landscape itself. There are some walks I take regularly, and keep my hand in by writing something every day, by hand, even if it's just a grocery list. I think the act of writing is an "historic" occurrence that happens in time and place with yourself, the writer, in a recorded moment. It's a very pure, unencumbered intersection, and when the words happen they are out of the realm of "good" or "bad" writing. It's a non-judgmental state. "First thought, best thought" is the oft-quoted phrase by Allen Ginsberg, which sums it up.

You've been writing some "political" poems in recent years.

I've felt since the 2000 election that there was a moral obligation to not "look the other way." I think it's important to articulate political observations, with some kind of humor and balance, and refuse to be victimized by the corrupt, corporate, buy-your-vote place the country is currently in. Locally, certainly in West Marin, people are very active politically, but in a larger overview there is little education on how global politics and economy affect us all. I'm thinking again of Allen Ginsberg, who as a political poet was able to use humor and outrage with an enormous amount of political detective information and skill. He named all the ills that are still here a generation later. We think times change, but a new generation grows up and sees the problems of the environment and economy are still very much here. Unfortunately.

The new National Poetry Foundation collection of your life's work is something of a landmark for you, isn't it?

It's always interesting to see if 40-some years of writing hangs together as a life's narrative. What exactly is that story about? I believe in chronology, and all my poems are dated. So the book flows like a journal. I think when my first book came out it was really exciting, but I have never found the publication of a book has changed my life much. The important thing, as Philip Whalen kept telling me, is to "just keep on writing. On the days it isn't fun, do something else."

In her introduction to your latest collection, Linda Russo writes, "Kyger returns us to 'where we are.'" What does "where we are" mean to you?

Awareness of the place you are in. Once you "know" one place, you know every place with that same intimate regard, from the ground up. Like the doe with her fawn eating birdseed scattered on the feeding table, whose mother taught her a few years earlier how to do it, and now she's teaching her baby the same habit. Bad habit. Big wet deer tongue marks on the wood surface.

About Now

This mooching doe
munching the fallen apples
from the tree outside the door
doesn't even bother to move

When I approach her suggesting
she exit which she does apple
still in mouth bounding
across the overgrazed wild sweet peas

About now
tiny iridescent
        pieces of abalone

        So intimate these overcast days

Home is the moment
the quail arrive

July 23, 2004

Giethoorm and Staphorst

Village Life Observed: Photography and Stories by Annet Held

HOLLAND, CIRCA 1950

Annet Held and her camera

IN THE 1950s I photographed these two villages situated in the north of Holland, only 20 miles apart (and 20 miles from the village in which I grew up), but they are two different worlds. "The Elders" and "Boatbuilder" are from Giethoorm, a very old settlement in the middle of lakes and wetlands, only accessible by boat or bike. The population is Protestant, but of a very open-minded variety. In the 1950s they chose as their minister a homosexual who lived with his Italian boyfriend in the rectory. The people never regretted their choice, and the minister stayed for years.

Staphorst is less isolated, but people there live in a totally closed society, with strict rules for all matters of everyday life. They dress as they have for hundreds of years. They are excellent farmers.

Staphorst Interior

The village is a visual pleasure, the houses thatch-roofed with green doors, the interiors like 17th-century Dutch paintings. The walls are tiled, the floor is stone, and every Saturday white sand is scattered on the floors to protect them from people's wooden shoes.

Annet Held

Jan Schreur, Boatbuilder in Giethoorm

Jan Schreur's family built these types of boats for hundreds of years, and they continue to do so. Jan heats and wets the wood in order to bend it.

Giethoorm Elders

When I took this photo, the old lady asked me how much I was going to pay her. I told her I wouldn't pay her, but I would send her a copy of the photo, which I did.

Annet Held

Love in Staphorst

In Staphorst in the 1950s, a teenage girl would carry a little embroidered bag to market. If she allowed a boy to have the bag, she would be waiting for him the following Thursday night. Their secret meetings continued until the girl was pregnant, then both families arranged a wedding.

Oblique Tide

Donald Bacon

Low tide drains to extreme—exposing

random rows of white, off-white iridescent oyster stakes
riddling the outer rim of mudflats
in Hamlet Pen.
They prick the waterline, probe oxide mud—glittering
spikes, splinters, slivers, mere nicks of light.

An egret sparks the cordgrass
titanium white.

ındee's Restaurant
7824 Covert Ln
Sebastopol, CA
(707) 829-2642

Check #: 3602	10/5/16
Server: Maile K	5:47 PM
Table: T11/8	Guests: 1
1 Salmon Lyonnaise	18.00
ADD TO MEAL: Green Salad	2.50
Sub-total	20.50
Sales Tax	1.95
TOTAL	22.45
Balance Due	22.45

Thank You!

Andeo's Restaurant
7824 Covert Ln
Sebastopol, CA
(707) 829-2642

Check #: 3602	10/5/16
Server: Malie K	5:47 PM
Table: 11/8	Guests: 1

1 Salmon Lyonnaise	18.00
ADD TO MEAL: Green Salad	2.50

Sub-total	20.50
Sales Tax	1.95
TOTAL	22.45

Balance Due	22.45

Thank You!

Donald Bacon

Halfway out across the flats a zone of isolating mud
squeezes ribs
out of a hulk of sunken pier on cross-plank beams and pilings.
The long cargo wharf once jutting out from Preston Point
wrinkled into driftwood.

Skeleton of caged sun—
salt-torched, peroxide-gray, pickled raw,
timbers of wharf sag on stumps of molting creosote and brine,
silting under a slough of muck and mercury tailings
flushed down Walker Creek.

Remaindered, so irresolute—stilts and stakes relive
the rotting drag of each hour's tide.

Windowpane and frame. Paradigm—
a brushstroke away.
Acrylic crackles
the world of canvas into ignited, ambivalent white.

Obliquity's the clearest light.

Kathleen P. Goodwin, *South from Sculptured Beach,* 2003, watercolor, 9 x 12 inches

Imagining Cherry Pie

Barbara Heenan

WHEN MY personal gods are smiling on me, when things are really going my way, I am likely to start getting messages on my home phone, beginning some time around George Washington's birthday and lasting not more than a couple of precious weeks. To anyone else they might sound like crank calls. There is the sound of chatter and laughing, clinking glasses and clattering plates, and then two familiar voices raised in a loud sing-song, belting out in unison the two words, "Cherry pie!" And the line goes dead.

It's Jim and Carol, who together have accrued more than twenty years of waiting tables at Tony's Seafood Restaurant in Marshall, California, telling those who don't know to seat themselves, greeting the regulars with special affection, and serving up sagging paper plates of bar-b-qued oysters. Now designated as one of the "thousand places to see before I die," Tony's has been patronized for decades by a range of locals—West Marin dairy ranchers, Inverness Yacht Club sailors, reclusive artists scattered in bungalows from Bolinas to Bodega, and even a United States senator visiting her weekend home in Stinson Beach.

The usual dessert menu at Tony's is cheesecake, apple pie, or vanilla ice cream, none of which interests me much. Only once a year does cherry pie appear, an occurrence as anxiously awaited by me as the herring run is by the few remaining fishermen on Tomales Bay. I know not to expect herring in August or cherry pie in June. But I can't help but ask, on the frequent Friday nights we drive Route One along the east shore of the bay to the restaurant, where we will watch the light on the water, drink cheap white wine, and eat fresh fish, "Do you have cherry pie tonight?"

Neither Jim nor Carol has ever questioned me about my passion for cherry pie. Rather, like the friends they have become over many years, they accept me and my idiosyncrasy with grace. It was Jim, not one inclined to waste effort, who came up with the idea of calling me when it was on the menu. This strategy, he reasoned, might relieve us all from unnecessary and inevitably disappointing, dead-end conversations about what's for dessert at Tony's.

The cherry pie I want is not healthful. It's not what I crave if it isn't made out of canned, processed sour cherries topped with red-dye gelatinous goo, or if it's not wrapped in thick crust made from bleached white flour and bricks of lard. The cherry pie I like reminds me of Oklahoma where I grew up, the cafes in small towns like Mustang or El Reno or Kingfisher where my dad and grandfather and I meandered almost every Sunday in the family Buick. My cherry pie belongs under a yellowing plastic pie cover, sitting on the lunch counter not far from the cash register. It belongs on the plates of the old men dressed in blue-jean overalls wearing cowboy hats sweated through at the crowns and pink-and-turquoise plaid Western shirts frayed and faded at the cuffs, who slouch over their dessert, their huge mongrel hands scooping forkfuls in one continuous motion from plate to mouth. They drink coffee and smoke cigarettes and eat pie and talk garrulously, as comfortable in their skins as a herd of feeding cattle. I am not more than six or seven years old, and I rarely speak to any of the men, including my dad or my granddad. I just watch and listen.

The excuse for our Sunday drives was to look for the horse Dad and Granddad had promised me. For years we traveled mostly north and west of Oklahoma City, following the square grid of county roads, searching out barbed-wire gates and rutted tire tracks that led to the dirt farm where some old timer had advertised "Horses 4 Sale." Most often the horses were knock-kneed or sway-backed. But we got out of the car anyway, flushing half-plucked chickens and gawking kids in our path as we walked up to the front door of a wooden shack or a lopsided trailer propped on cement blocks. Sometimes, sometimes not, a man emerged to talk. It was then that my granddad, tall, handsome, white-haired, and Irish, acknowledged by all fifteen of his siblings as a connoisseur of women, goats, and horses, took the lead. Some conversations lasted only a moment or two. Some wandered on for hours, moving from the front stoop to the barn to a pasture of dust and dried thistles.

Inevitably, we moved on, back into the car and out to the paved road where the Buick's tires smacked in a reassuring syncopation over the lines of black tar that seemed to hold Oklahoma country roads together. We saw our share of cottonmouths and rattlesnakes and tarantulas, and scrub oaks black against tall yellow grass, and enormous cumulus towers build in the big-top sky. There were always more little towns, Yukon and Okarche, Calumet and Arcadia, their names still resonating in my ear not in standard English but in the mother tongue, an Okie twang that lingers on the "ewes" and the "ales." We drove slowly up their main streets, only occasionally stopping for coffee and a bite to eat.

If I am buck-naked honest, as Granddad would have said, I don't think I ever actually ate cherry pie in any of those small-town cafes. But cherry pie is as rooted in the landscape for me as the oil derricks and the pickup trucks, the tumbleweeds, and the noble red tails standing sentry every half-mile high atop their telephone-pole lookouts. Even today,

Anne Vitale, *57 Argyle: Vignettes of Home,* c. 1986/87, pen-and-ink, 6 x 6 inches

some 50 years later, I still see my father and grandfather from the back seat of our old sedan, their heads shaped exactly the same, broad and square and thick with hair.

I don't know if they continued scouting country roads and places after I started shaving my legs and teasing my hair. I don't think so. I do know I started noticing things in Oklahoma I had not seen when I was younger. On a junior high school field trip, our bus stopped in Paul's Valley, where we walked past a decrepit water fountain labeled "Colored" to use a cleaner, brighter one labeled "White." Out cruising past the city limits, a boyfriend and I were stopped short by an overturned watermelon truck, hundreds of split and bleeding melons blocking the road, and a horde of tow-headed, barefoot children scavenging what they could in the cooking summer heat. And on November 22, 1963 two of my classmates, Kent and Bill, always cool and carefully dressed in khaki slacks and light-blue buttondown oxford cloth shirts, jumped out of their desk chairs, cheering, when they heard that Kennedy was shot dead.

At 17 I ran as far and as fast as I could, never imagining that in my lifetime I could ever find a place to fit. Nor, back then, could I imagine ever longing for cherry pie. Today, sitting at our favorite table at Tony's, watching the bright riffles of waves on the water and wrapping my arm around a cherished slice of pie, I savor the wonder of finding both.

Fariba Bogzaran, *Invisible Dialogue,* 2007, acrylic on canvas, 36 x 48 inches

Fog

Barbara Lovejoy

Fog on the road,
cars ahead of me vanish—
will I also disappear?

Kehoe Beach Haiku

Gary Thorp

With no one to see it,
this solitary beetle
heads toward the sea

Letter from the Everglades

Karen Gray

APRIL, 2007—I dreamed of honeybees last night. There is a colossal, black, shiny bumblebee here that buzzes around the mangroves. Watching her set me to worrying about our honeybees at home. I was concerned for them after the severe freeze we had in February, so I wasn't surprised when I began to hear about a die-off observed in California. But then the story got more complicated: bees all over the country were not returning to their hives. One day the beekeeper would check inside the hives and everything looked fine. The next day—no bees. Not dead or dying in the hive. Absent.

Before we left on this trip to the Gulf of Mexico I sat under our blooming apple tree in the garden with my tea and the newspaper on a sunny Sunday. The quiet was eerie. I looked up into the blossoms and saw one honeybee on her rounds. There should have been hundreds setting up a constant hum in the flower canopy as the petals twitched with their activity.

Honeybees are my California, as essential to the nature of the place as the earth and sky. One of my most vivid early memories is of watching and listening as a honeybee worked her way into a silken California poppy, collected the pollen granules, and emerged from her labors heavily dusted in the rich stuff ready for take-off to the next blossom.

Bees are melded in my memory with warmth, sunshine, and food. Always with food, because the food in our fields and orchards wouldn't grow without the bees. I don't imagine that anyone ever told me that. I think I just always understood it. We grew alfalfa, almonds, peaches, and grapes. The whitewashed wooden boxes of bees sat stacked crookedly at the ends of the rows every spring, as much a part of the ranch as the workers who pruned and the ditches that delivered the irrigation water. Bees were everywhere: in the fields, in the hot canning shed in summer attracted by the sweet smell of freshly made jam, fighting against the screens inside the house where they were trapped and in need of shooing back outdoors again to do their job, buzzing around our heads in the car looking for the way back out the window as we whizzed along country roads. Through all of my childhood shared with honeybees, I was never stung once.

When I was grown and had moved to Point Reyes, my husband kept bees on our grassy hill. He shared the harvesting equipment for the honey with two other local beekeepers. When he failed to put a super on the hive fast enough for the growing colony to expand one season, they swarmed into our upstairs bedroom through a crack in the roof. The other beekeepers came over and helped to capture the swarm, taking it to a new hive box to establish a new colony.

It was a sad day when we had to give them up. My neighbor was allergic to bee stings and couldn't abide them living so close to her. Later, when I saw bees working in my garden I would wonder where their home was, how far they had traveled to work that day. Now I wonder if they will make it back home again at all.

POINT REYES
FARMSTEAD
CHEESE COMPANY
www.pointreyescheese.com

La Vida

Students, Marin Literacy Photography Project and Gallery Route One

POINT REYES STATION

***Dos Mundos*/Two Worlds**
Imelda Macias, 2008
Hoy en día cuando tengo la cámara en mis manos no me siento tímida.
With the camera in my hands, I don't feel shy.

DESDE EL 2003, Gallery Route One en Point Reyes Station y el Proyecto de Alfabetización en West Marin han patrocinado una clase de fotografía enseñada por la fotógrafa periodísta, Luz Elena Castro. Los alumnos de ESL (English as a Second Language) se reunen con los voluntarios de la Galeria de Arte para crear ehibiciones bilingues en temas que tocan la vida de los fotógrafos novatos. La exhibición del año 2008, de donde éstas imágenes han sido sacadas, fue titulada La Vida: Trabajo y Familia.

SINCE 2003, Gallery Route One in Point Reyes Station has sponsored a photography class led by photojournalist Luz Elena Castro. The class brings Marin Literacy Project's English students together with Gallery volunteers to create annual bilingual exhibits on themes touching the novice photographers' lives. The 2008 show from which these images are drawn was titled *La Vida: Trabajo y Familia.*

Maricela Mora, *Marta y María a La Quesería/ Marta and María at the Cheese Factory*, 2008

Trabajo Satisfactorio/Satisfying Work

Juanita Romo, 2008

Aprender fotografía me ha demostrado que puedo ser más en ésta vida que sólo un ama de casa.
Photography has shown me I can be more in this life than just a housewife.

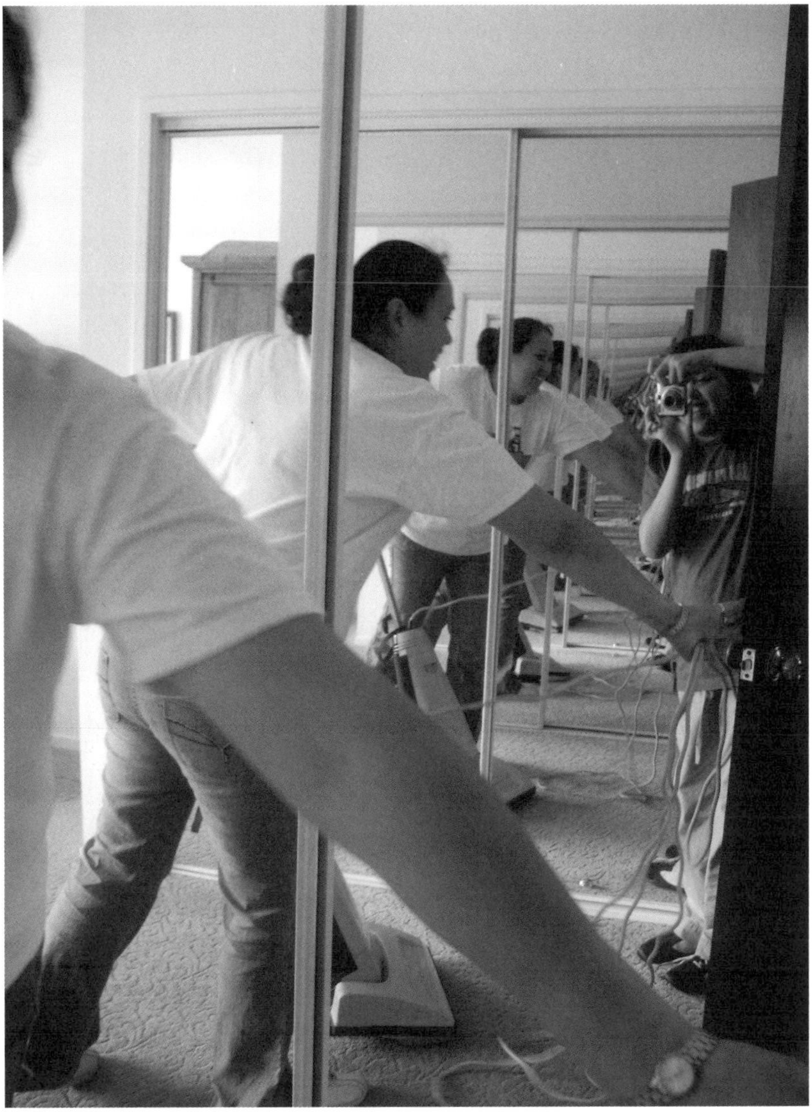

Reflexión/Reflection

Alejandra Macías, 2008

Mamá, mira cuantas Alejandras hay!
Mama, look how many Alejandras there are!

Silverton

Rosaleen Bertolino

NATHAN'S MOTHER called out to his grandmother, "I'll miss you!" and blew a kiss. Then, the minute she got in the car, muttered, "Jesus. I thought that visit would never end." She backed the car down the driveway as his grandmother, in a pink top and green pants, waved from the doorway.

Nathan himself had enjoyed seeing his grandmother, the only grandparent he had, whom he had visited only once before. Because of the desert heat, she kept the shades down all day—and the dimness and the pale green paint of the walls gave him a pleasurable and spooky feeling of living inside an aquarium. She showed him photos of his mother as a little girl, her hair in ribbons, sitting at the upright piano that was still in the living room, and in high school with her hair teased into a pile, a beehive, they called it.

"She ran away once," his grandmother told him.

"Why?" Nathan asked, feeling queasy.

"She was wild."

"Not true," said his mother. "I couldn't wait to leave town, though."

His mother would not go near the piano, claiming she was rusty. But Nathan's grandmother sat down and banged out "You Are My Sunshine."

"You have a natural talent!" his grandmother said when Nathan fiddled with the glossy keys. Her large, white false teeth gleamed in her seamed face.

Kurt Lai, *Reflection*, 2008

Last night, he had helped his grandmother make a tortilla casserole. As she bent close, explaining how to layer the chips, he smelled something rotten. His grandmother's breath made him want to get away, and yet he loved her.

Thinking that this was why his mother had been glad to leave, he said, "Grandma has bad breath."

"It's the dentures," replied his mother, merging the car onto the highway. "God, I thought she'd never stop talking. I know she means well, but I have enough to worry about without her analyzing every little thing I do. Light me a cigarette, will you?"

He pulled a cigarette from the pack of Camels on the seat between them and pushed in the cigarette lighter, then held the orange coil to the tip of the cigarette until it lit.

She took it from him with her right hand, passed it to her left, inhaled greedily, and blew the smoke in a swift plume toward the window. The air outside sucked up the smoke, an invisible mouth.

"Will you have a job when we get back?" She worked at the Raley's, ringing up people's groceries.

"Of course," she said tensely. "They know I'm on vacation."

They were headed back home, a two-day drive from eastern Nevada to the coast of California. The lunch his grandmother had packed for them sat in a paper bag on top of their suitcases in the backseat. The sun, a brilliant fire at the horizon behind them, was just rising as they reached the outskirts of town.

The highway was flat as a tabletop, surrounded by dusty brown, nothing to see but scrub and dirt, frightening in its vastness.

"What if our car breaks down?" he asked, remembering a time when it had, along a freeway, and sitting locked in the car for what seemed hours while his mother hiked to the off-ramp for help. "No one lives here."

"We won't break down," his mother said firmly, but Nathan wasn't so sure.

In the distance, a wall of hazy blue mountains.

"Can we play Twenty Questions?"

His answer was "Sparkles," their next-door-neighbor's Jack Russell terrier, whom he adored, and which she correctly guessed by question ten. Hers was "cloud," which he did not guess, although he came close with "smoke."

They reached the tan foothills and, as they began to climb, played the game where they guessed the color of the next approaching vehicle.

"Red," he said.

"White," she said.

The truck that roared past was black.

"Blue."

"Silver."

She gasped as their car bumped and swerved.

"What happened?"

"We ran over a piece of tire," she said sternly, glancing in the rearview mirror. "Now please be quiet. I need to concentrate."

"How did the tire get in the road?"

"I don't know."

He studied his mother's freckled hands, the way they clenched the steering wheel, white at the knuckles, and, when the road straightened out again, how they expertly removed flakes of tobacco from her lips. Unlike his friends' mothers, she did not wear lipstick.

"Why don't you wear lipstick?" he asked her.

"I don't have the mouth for it."

"What is the right kind of mouth?"

"Not mine. Stop asking so many questions. Anyone would think you were four, not seven."

He sat on his hands to remind himself to keep quiet. She did not like people who talked too much, such as his grandmother. She liked it quiet. Russell, a man she had dated, became too loud and she had gotten rid of him fast.

Her nose had a bump at the top. Near the outside corner of her right eye, freckles clustered so thickly they melted together into a tiny puddle. Her blonde eyebrows were fine, nearly invisible; she wore black mascara and eyeliner. Her eyes were ocean blue, her hair strawberry blonde, smoothed into a ponytail. He thought her beautiful.

The road began spiraling up the mountain and his mother kept both hands on the wheel. He held her cigarettes, lifting them to her mouth when she wanted the next puff.

Near the top, where there were patches of snow although it was July, they stopped for lunch. His mother plunged their cans of cola into a clump of snow to chill them, delighting Nathan. As he ate a ham sandwich and potato chips, he listed other uses for snow: "Bee stings…snow cones…ice-packs! We could collect the snow and sell it."

His mother shook her head. "They can manufacture snow, silly."

"But this would be the real thing," said Nathan. "Mountain snow."

On the descent, he became carsick and she pulled off the road. While he heaved next to a leafless shrub, she stood over him with her cool hand on the nape of his neck.

"Are you done?"

He nodded.

"Let's go then, I want to get to Silverton before dark."

She didn't like to drive at night. "The lights hurt my eyes," she had told him once.

Silverton, where she had reserved a motel room, was halfway home. He liked the sound of it, "silver, ton." He imagined a place full of silver, heaps of it. He dozed.

When he woke, they were driving through orchards, the trees in rows like pieces on an endless checkerboard, their slender trunks painted white at the bottom.

"Why are they white?"

"I don't know. Probably it keeps them healthy. Maybe it's like socks."

"Tree socks?"

"Right."

"What kind of trees?"

"Fruit. Hand me a cigarette, would you?"

"What kind of fruit?"

"How the hell would I know? I'm not a farmer!"

She was in a bad mood. They'd been driving all day and she wanted to stop and rest. "Now be quiet for a while," she said. "You're such a chatterbox."

Chastised, he gazed out the window at the orderly trees, so different from the sparse desert shrubs, the irregular clumps of mountain pines.

At last they reached Silverton. They crossed a steel bridge, whose base clattered under their tires. Under the bridge a green river flowed. They went through a neighborhood of little houses in pastel colors, a tidy downtown. The road curved around a small lake sprinkled with a few brightly colored pedal boats. Children splashed in the water.

"Can we stop?"

She sighed.

"Just for a minute?"

She parked the car. While she smoked at a picnic table, Nathan took off his shoes, rolled up his pants, and waded into the cool water. A few yards away a rope line of orange floats indicated where the water became deep.

"Don't go past that line!" his mother shouted, as though he were too little to understand about danger.

He ignored her, hoping that people would think she was shouting at someone else.

The warm mud sucked at his toes. Something silvery flickered past him in the water. He stepped forward to follow it, felt the surprise of pain. His blood swirled like smoke. He'd cut his foot.

He limped up the bank to her.

"My foot," he said, holding it up. His lower lip trembled as he tried to hold the tears in. It hurt worse now that he was next to her.

"Let me see." She bent close. "What happened?"

"I stepped on something."

"I see that." She kissed his cheek and he squirmed away, not wanting her to treat him like a baby.

At the motel, his mother made him undress and take a shower. He yelped as the water ran over his cut, stinging.

"Can I be finished?"

"No!" She frowned. "I can't remember when you last had a tetanus shot."

"Why would I need a shot?"

"Let's worry about it later," she said, holding out a towel.

They bought hamburgers, fries, and root beer floats at the A&W drive-in. As they ate, he listed the reasons why they should get a dog: "Protection from robbers, protection from kidnappers, plus you will know when someone is at the door." She didn't get irritated as she usually did when he brought up the subject of dogs.

Ashley Howze, *Untitled*, 2008, mixed media collage on masonite, 7 x 7 inches

"Nathan, they're too much work," she said finally.

"I'll take care of it," he promised.

"We'll see," she said, and hope surged through him.

Back in the motel room, while she took a shower, he jumped on the bed, which was nice and springy. He played with the air conditioner's controls, opened and closed the blinds. An elderly couple strolling past turned and stared at him as the blinds sprang open.

"Stop that," said his mother, towel wrapped around her hair, her skin flushed.

Halfway through *Jeopardy,* his mother began rummaging through her purse.

"Dammit," she said, "I was sure I had another pack." She stood up.

"Don't open the door to anyone," she said. "What did I say?"

"Don't open the door."

"Don't answer the door, either," she said. "I'll be back in a few minutes."

He began to worry about an hour after she'd left, when he'd finished watching *The Brady Bunch* and *The Odd Couple* and she had not returned. He peeked through the blinds, looking for her car, wondering what he should do. He walked around the room, stepping onto the bed and marching across the mattress as though it was a trail that led him to her cosmetics bag on the bureau. He sniffed at her skin lotion, Jergen's. A cowboy movie came on and he settled down to watch it.

Nathan felt anxious again when the 11 o'clock news came on and she was still gone. She had promised to be back in a few minutes.

There was, of course, the time she had promised not to kill the spider running across the floor, but had squashed it anyway, when she thought he wasn't looking. And other times, such as when she told him that he would like Russell when he got to know him, or that he would like creamed spinach if he would only taste it, but he did not and did not. So she could have been lying. He hoped so, even though it made him angry. Because otherwise he did not understand what could have happened to her.

Perhaps she had gone for cigarettes, and the store had had an emergency: a man having a heart attack, or an old lady falling down, cracking her skull. Maybe robbers had burst in: his mother stood in the store with her hands up. Perhaps she had been shot. His heart pounded at this scenario, the sort he liked to play at in games: policeman or robber or cowboy, he liked to point his finger and squeeze the trigger. He heard whimpering, then realized that he was the one making the noise.

This is a nice town, he told himself, remembering the pretty lake, trying to reassure himself, as she would have if she had been there. Perhaps the car had broken down. She had had to hike miles for help, wait for the tow truck, and so on. Dealing with car trouble could take a long time.

He turned the knob from channel to channel, trying to find something soothing. He settled on a talk show. He watched the actors crossing their legs and tossing their heads back, the secret language of grown-ups in these coded gestures. At home she often left him while she went to the store for cigarettes or milk, but she had never been gone long. He wondered if she was trying to teach him a lesson. He asked too many questions and this was the punishment: to wait, quietly, alone.

He didn't begin to cry until after he had fallen asleep without meaning to, and woke to the television crackling with snow, and she was still not there. But the crying was strange, his jaw stiff, the tears squeezed out. He knew already that crying would not bring her back, and soon he stopped.

When the sun came up, he ate the potato chips and the red licorice he found in the grocery bag. Later, he drank water to keep his stomach full. The morning passed in a haze. He heard the maids wheeling their carts along the concrete walkway outside the rooms. They shouted at one another in a foreign language.

Finally, one of them unlocked the door.

He was asked the same questions over and over again, first by the motel owner, then by the police.

"Where did she say she was going?"

"Did she leave a note?"

"Did she seem upset?

The last question bothered him because he did not know the answer. How upset? he wanted to ask them. Instead he said, "She went to buy cigarettes."

His grandmother came and took him back to Nevada. This time the dim light of his grandmother's house made him feel empty. The desert heat pressed down on him, flattening his thoughts into ribbons, until they turned to smoke and vanished altogether. His grandmother lowered her voice when she talked on the phone. Still, he caught snatches. "Vanished...No one knows...no body...no car." The cut on his foot became infected, the glands around his neck swollen. It became hard to breathe.

"Tetanus," the doctor said.

He drank his meals through a straw. By the time he was better again and ready to start his new school, he had become used to not speaking. Words stumbled out clumsily, in a sputter. And in the end, because of all the questions, it became safer to be quiet.

"Where are you from?" the kids at school asked.

"Why do you live with your grandma?"

"Where're your parents?"

In answer to all of these, he shrugged. He became as quiet as he had once been talkative. On the walk home from school, which took him past a dusty park with a tire swing and a metal jungle gym that was too hot to touch, a group of boys lounged.

"Are you mental?" the tallest asked him.

Nathan shook his head.

"I'd say you are."

They pushed him into the dirt. Nathan lay limply as they kicked and pummeled, receiving the blows as if he deserved them. Soon they ran off.

"Good Lord," his grandmother said. "You were in a fight."

Nathan shrugged. Telling her would break the agreement he'd made to stay closed, waiting, until his mother returned and his real life could begin again.

Later, when he was lying on the webbed recliner outside the back door with a small piece of meat she'd cut from a steak pressed to one eye, she asked, "Would you like to take piano lessons?"

He bolted upright as though fending off an assault. "No!"

"I won't make you."

She had become quiet, too. Her slippered feet dragged as she shuffled away, making a scratchy sandpaper sound. Her hair, formerly a strawberry blonde puff, had gone flat and gray at the roots. She did not sit down at the piano to play "You Are My Sunshine." She no longer told him funny stories of when she worked at the casino or of his mother's childhood.

The desert sky was larger than in California and, at night, heavy with stars. Although his mother was the one who had vanished, it was Nathan and his grandmother who seemed under a spell. They drifted through their days, polite to one another in the manner of the disengaged, as if in a state of suspended animation.

When he had nightmares, she let him sleep in her bed. She made spaghetti and sandwiches with the crusts cut off.

The television blared from morning to night, always lively, scandalized, hopeful. Breakfast was *The Jack LaLanne Show* and *Sesame Street.* After dinner, they watched detective shows, *Hawaii Five-O, The FBI, Kojak.* The detectives pulled clues together and solved the mystery.

On his own, pulling together bits and pieces, Nathan constructed an explanation for his mother's disappearance. She had gotten amnesia (by bumping her head) but as soon as she was cured (by another bump on the head), she would, of course, return.

He was eight, nine, and ten, and she did not.

One evening, gathering up his courage, and waiting until there was a commercial, he asked his grandmother, as casually as he could, "Do you know why she left?"

His grandmother looked at him, startled. "You do know it's not your fault, dear," she said. "You must know that at least."

But that was the thing he did not know at all. Nevertheless, he nodded and they turned toward the television once more. He thought his mother might have grown tired of her life with him and run away—to Alaska or Hawaii. He wondered about his father, about why he'd never met him. "Love is blind," his mother had told him, shaking her head. Maybe she had come to believe that he, like his father, was a mistake. He left for school each morning but did not always end up there; sometimes he found himself at the park, where he leaned against a birch and when the lunch bell rang, opened up the paper bag and ate his sandwich.

He was eleven, twelve, thirteen.

At fourteen, lying on his bed, he fingered the pack of cigarettes he'd bought from the liquor store down the street. "They're for my mother," he'd told the man.

He was curious. Desire for cigarettes had taken her out of the motel room. Smoking, at first, was like unlocking a door: this was what it had felt like when she'd inhaled, and like this when she'd tapped the ash. But by claiming cigarettes for himself, his memories of his mother dimmed further. The smell, gestures, rituals became his, and what he remembered of her began to seem imaginary. He liked the buzz of nicotine, the hot rush of smoke into his lungs. Smoking was something a quiet person could do in company. He simultaneously hardened and softened as the smoke swirled into his lungs; feeling more confident when he smoked, he relaxed.

"I don't know what you think you're accomplishing," his grandmother said when she caught him.

"You don't know anything," he said.

She pressed her lips together bleakly. "You're becoming just like her," she said. "God help us."

He stalked out of the house. It was scorching out, and the heat burned into him. The little park was closed for repairs, but he scaled the chain-link fence and sat in the shade of the birches.

Lately, he had become obsessed with the idea of a phone call. He believed that would be how she would make contact, it would seem safer to her than a visit. Her voice would be low, hoarse from years of smoking, and hesitant.

"Nathan?"

"Yes?"

"It's me, your mother."

He would say nothing because nothing was what she deserved.

"I'm hoping we could meet."

He would hang up, of course. It was the only possible response. Each time he played this out in his head, he felt victorious, and miserable. He did not need her; he needed no one. The leaves of the birch trees fluttered overhead like little hands. The breeze was like hot breath grazing his face. He felt restless and thought he might leave. It's how we do things, he thought, my mother and I. We move on. The interstate wasn't far; he could hear the ocean sounds of its traffic from here. He could walk out there tonight and catch a ride.

He slipped in the back door, hoping to avoid his grandmother in the living room; she watched *The Mike Douglas Show* this time of day. But she was at the kitchen table, waiting for him. The television was silent and her cheeks were wet.

"Sit down," she said. "I've gotten a phone call."

A month ago, plagued with an invasion of mitten crabs, Silverton's public works department had dredged the town lake. At

Angelica Casey, *Untitled*, 2008, mixed media collage on masonite, 7 x 7 inches

the bottom of the lake, at its deepest part, was a car, in the car a woman's skeleton.

"I knew she'd never left on purpose," his grandmother said, wiping her eyes. But she had never said so before and he knew that was because she hadn't known. She tried to hug him and he stiffened in her arms.

Late that night, he returned to the park. He stumbled jumping down from the fence, feeling sore and stunned, as he had years ago when the boys had beaten him up, and, the same now as then, as if he deserved this. He did not know how to erase the stories he had told himself about her over the years, now lodged inside him like tumors: how she'd run off to escape him, how she'd hidden herself as punishment.

"We're going to Silverton," his grandmother had said.

"What's the point?"

She'd slapped him, the first time ever that she'd touched him in anger. He could have easily pushed her down, or he could simply leave, as planned, heading out to the interstate.

"She's your mother."

"Was."

The sky was layers of clouds and half a moon. He'd always imagined her alive. The police in Silverton were idiots. Seven years to figure out that she had never left town. He pressed his hands against a tree trunk; papery curls crumbled under his palms. He and his grandmother were idiots, too. If love made any difference, they should have known she was right there all along.

His grandmother was a slow driver. Her Buick crept along the highway. The mountain roads, their shoulders piled with hard, dirty snow, made her nervous, and she slowed further. As they crawled past granite boulders, Nathan's heart clenched like a fist. This might have been where he and his mother had picnicked. There, possibly, he had gotten carsick. He wanted to jump out of the car.

In defiance of his grandmother, he rolled down his window and lit a cigarette.

"There's no need to be frightened," she said.

In response, he attempted a sneer but halfway through his face crumpled. He curled toward the window. He hadn't expected that tears would feel good.

By the time they arrived in Silverton it was night. The bridge clattered under their tires. The lake water glittered innocently in the moonlight.

The next morning, at the coroner's office, he and his grandmother were given a large metal box containing his mother's remains. A muscular police officer took them around the back of the station so that they could see the rusty car, encrusted with freshwater clamshells and dry strands of moss algae. He showed them, too, the purse that had once been red, its vinyl crackled, a lumpy object that had once been a wallet, and the two packs of cigarettes, still sealed in cellophane. He had a faint air of apology in his voice that contrasted oddly with his swagger. "The windows were open," he said. "The car sank quickly."

He turned to Nathan. "Did she seem despondent that night?"

His grandmother bristled. "He was seven," she said.

"I'm sorry."

With the box containing his mother in the backseat, Nathan and his grandmother drove to the lake and stood at the water's edge. He had returned here thousands of times over the years, trying to solve the mystery of his mother, yet never once had he imagined this.

The dredging work finished, the lake was as pretty as the first time he'd seen it, the green water a sheet of silk, a row of bright orange and blue pedal boats tied up to a little dock. A family picnicked on the opposite bank and a dog splashed at the edge of the water.

"Don't let what he said bother you," said his grandmother, her puff of hair lifting in the breeze. "There could have been a deer crossing the road."

"Or a dog," he said, suddenly understanding that it was up to them to choose the story.

They began the drive home, past precise miles of fruit trees. Nathan found himself turning frequently to gaze at the box that held his mother in the back seat. His hand crept toward it and rested on the metal.

By late afternoon they had reached the mountains, winding up and up, through tall, dark pines, then short, sparse trees, and finally enormous slabs of granite and sky.

Here his mother had chilled their colas, twisting the cans deep into the icy crystals, then stretched her freckled arms high above her head as he had scrambled from boulder to boulder.

Nathan cleared his throat. "She never wore lipstick," he remarked, feeling light and giddy, at the highest point in the arc of a swing.

Bolinas Lagoon

William Keener

Sink into a salt marsh. Walk out
and stand on black fragrant mud.

It will hold you, suck you down
with its slow viscous grip
until your rubber boots succumb.

Let your gaze go where it's deep,
past cordgrass and pickleweed,
where curlews press their runes
in newlaid silt, and bivalves
leave their bubbles in the ooze.

Watch the clouds cream up
in a cerulean sky, as the light
comes gliding in from the west
to land like a flock at your feet.

The ebb tide's last remaining
lamina of water makes the mud
a mirror where the avocets walk
with ease, each bird tipping
down to touch its upcurved bill.

And you can't take another step,
transfixed in the sumptuous muck.

Evvy Eisen, *The Oysterman*, 2008,
black-and-white silver gelatin print

A Textured Felt

Marilyn Longinotti Geary

From distant points,
lines converge, then merge,
here where land and ocean join.

From across the Aleutians, along continent edge,
trails twine down to Bauli-n.

Following the flanks of América del Sur,
threads of alpaca coil to the valley Chileno.

Fishing lines spanning the Earth's vast waters
hook the isle of Iz to Tomales Bay.

Ribbons of lace bind the Portuguese Azores
to Olema Valley's grass-covered pastures.

Cables of wool curl from the Emerald Isle
to Marshall's dry-farmed fields.

Silk strands stretch from Ticino's steep valleys
to Nicasio's rolling ranch lands.

From Jalostotitlán, near caves of sand,
cords of agave break through cracks in a border
covered in crosses for those died in passage.

Knotted, tangled, plied over time,
these disparate lines and myriads more,
crissed and crossed, converging here,
felt a fabric so tightly formed,
no single thread can be drawn out
without ripping the whole.

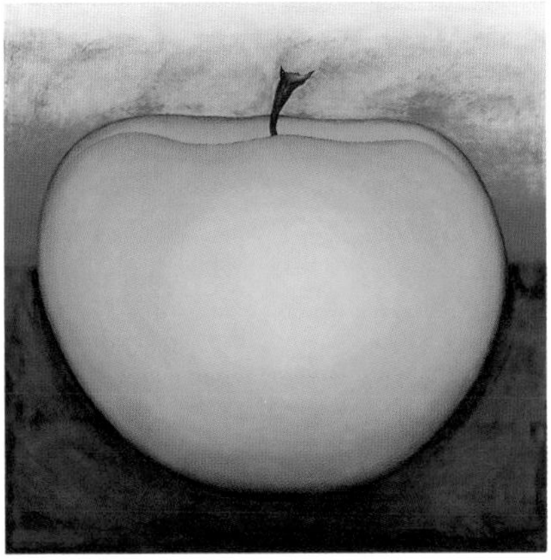

Louise Maloof, *Erika's Apple,* 2008, oil on
canvas with beeswax, 40 x 40 x 4 inches

Gale S. McKee, *Leaving Home,* 2006, acrylic and mixed-media on canvas, 40 x 32 inches

Things

Francine Allen

IN 1999, when my Uncle Sam was 82 years old, a can of ravioli exploded in his kitchen, embedding shrapnel into the ceiling. My brother, who cleaned up the mess, found the expiration date on the can: November 17, 1953. Uncle Sam had been 36 years old when he'd purchased that can of raviolis.

Sam accumulated in his house brown paper bags and cartons filled with hundreds of pens, pencils, pocket knives, useless keys and key chains, screwdrivers, tape measures, buttons, small electronic gadgets he'd never used, boxes of handkerchiefs and socks he'd never opened, newspaper clippings, photographs and letters, magazines, books, soaps, assorted cans and bottles of fruit and fruit juice, ketchup and pickle relish—so many things that only a narrow pathway led to his chair, a guest chair, the chair he used at the kitchen table, the bed, and the bathroom's toilet and sink—a path too narrow to push a vacuum cleaner through.

We were laughing about the ravioli story, my brother and I, as we cleaned out my uncle's bedroom. He had died three days before. My brother had already been through everything, probably grabbing all the good stuff, but I didn't begrudge him whatever he'd found. I've always been proud of my preference for simplicity.

Besides, he'd been the one who'd emptied out Sam's house the year before when Sam moved into my brother's spare bedroom. They had sifted through all of his belongings then and Sam took with him only what he really wanted to keep. Soon his bedroom looked a lot like his house had—only a path remained to the bed and closet, but considering he'd lived in a two-bedroom house with an attic and basement, he'd gotten rid of a lot: two large Dumpsters and three truckloads to Goodwill, to be exact.

So we were going through what was left of Sam's things, his final, winnowed holdings. And I found two things I could not throw away: an old Pall Mall cigarette tin that held a complete series of driver's licenses, his life captured in the photos, and a birthday card he received on his eighth birthday, the simple expression of his mother's love inscribed in my beloved grandmother's exquisite nineteenth-century handwriting. These were dear objects I wanted to keep.

Then my brother reached under Sam's bed.

"Do you remember this thing?" he asked, pulling out a ball of lead gum wrappers the size and weight of a cannonball.

He handed over what suddenly transformed into an extinguished meteor that had passed through space and time. This object held the weight of love; it was my still point in a turning world, my most precious object that I'd forgotten, that I'd never imagined seeing again.

"Do you want it?" I asked casually.

"No way," he scoffed.

He put the lead ball into my hands—so heavy, so magically weighty for its size. I am a young child again, rushing up the rickety wooden steps of my grandmother's house to rap my hand against its glass front door and peer along the edge of a moth-colored shade. I watch the fuzzy pink-and-blue shape that is my grandmother wobble down the hallway. Closer and closer she comes. Finally, the shade is pulled aside and my grandmother's face fills with her beautiful smile. She drags the warped door slowly against the floor and draws me gently into the soft pillow darkness of her breast.

Then, always, I run into the living room to lift an almost impossibly heavy ball, the weight I hold now: the treasure that Uncle Sam carried for me all this time.

A Dry Spring

Rick Lyttle

Last year we had a dry spring.

With March half over, I stripped
  and lay spread-eagle on the drive,
  face up, mouth wide open.

In the garden, Jean, being more practical,
  started watering.

Often when I heard the hose
  I thought it might be raining,
  but I was wrong day after day.

In May, with grass wilting
  and strong winds day and night,
  Jean said: *It's not working.*
  Why not come in now?
  No one can say you didn't try.

Dry spring, warm marriage.

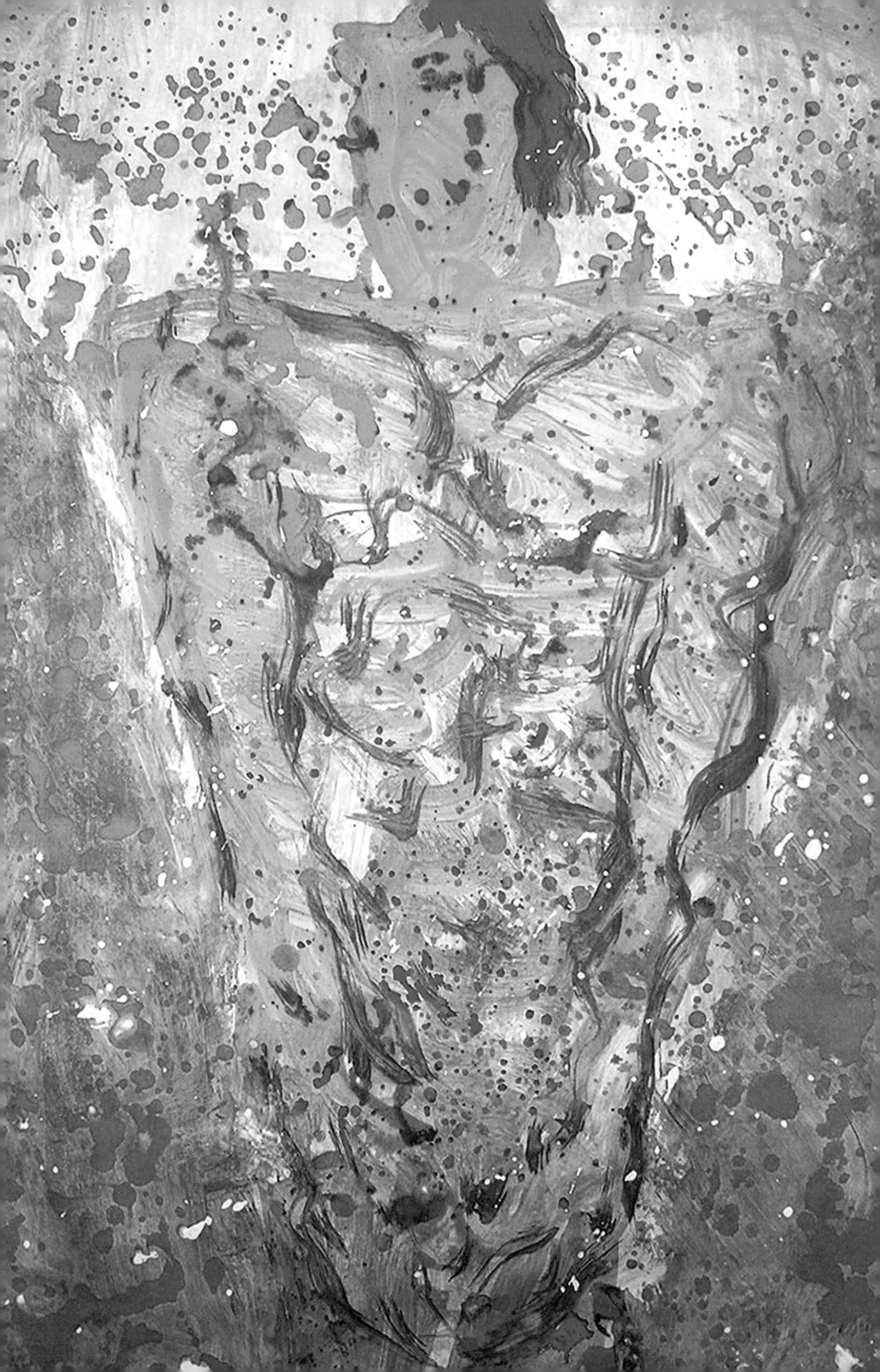

What Would Buddha Do?

Elizabeth Whitney

I JUST LEARNED that when you are facing someone going psycho, What would Buddha do? is the wrong question. The right question is: What would a psychiatric nurse do? I have no idea what Buddha would do, except that probably it would be something so mind-blowing that the person would calm down. Jesus, we have on record, would command, "Be gone, devils," and the devils would fly out of this poor tortured soul who is freaking out in front of me in my kitchen. Meanwhile, ordinary human me is trying to hold my ground and keep things from getting further out of hand. I'm in unknown territory.

Cause and effect are playing by different rules. Her overreaction is caused by my under-reaction. I am not living up to an illusion she manufactured. In her right mind she came to me as a house-sitter, but while she stayed at my house she gradually succumbed to the idea that when I came back I would let her stay and live with me. She is another wounded soul, gradually sliding down society's flagpole. She lost a job as a caregiver and became homeless. She is trying, without a phone, to get through the bureaucracy's hoops to qualify for disability status and being shoved out further and further by people who don't want her around. Somehow she acquired two dogs to keep her company; they all sleep in a Ford Fiesta. She is ruled by emotions and ruined by emotions.

But she can also be presentable and intelligent and erudite. She's read a lot of the books I have on metaphysics and religion. She can talk eloquently and quote from these books. She was thrilled to find in my

Claudia Chapline, *Swimmer in the Sun,* 2002, acrylic on paper, 32 x 22 inches little rented house a library of old friends—and art and beauty and a sweet yard with flowers to water and a fence all around to keep her two dogs safe. She got safe here. She found a friendly person here. She was regarded as a real person and reminded of herself, briefly, here. But then I came home and wanted her to move on. The dream was shattered and so was she, unable to reconcile the external reality of her exile to her imagined world of sanctuary found.

I watch her change and know I am in trouble. She is not what she seemed, and what's emerging is a full-on psychological disintegration. She's reduced to a blubbering child, wanting to know why I don't like her, won't let her stay in my storeroom where she will be very quiet, she promises, if only I won't make her go away where she is scared and can't sleep. She wants to know what is wrong with her, why I want her to go. She's screaming at me now, "I was fine! I was fine! Why did you start asking me those questions?"

She began changing when I introduced the subject of what she would do when she secured a place of her own, what skills she thought she could still use, since she could no longer do the bodywork she used to earn her living at, work that finally ruined her wrists and back. This question set off an alarm, it was the "plan" question that everyone asked her. She wanted to keep the conversation the way it was before, when we were comparing our lives and our influences: Dylan, Arguelles, the Buddhists, Hillman, Eckhart Tolle.

I'd had a long, long cycle of homeless survival. Twenty years of house-sitting and, as I preferred to call it, living outdoors, that ended three years ago when I finally came back to my rural village hometown. There were some islands of security in those years but it was mostly a big long swim across an ocean that required me to keep my head above water 24/7. I know the only reason I made it was that I was mentally and physically healthy. I have never made very much money, so the housing thing was impossible to hang on to. The more money I made, the higher the rents got, and finally I cast off the whole interface with that world and looked for another formula. California's long dry season makes this possible, and a lifetime of camping out makes it familiar, and years of doing it makes you good at it. As long as you don't lose your mind, which I apparently never did, because I was fully cognizant of the predicament I found myself in faced with a potentially dangerous and extremely disagreeable showdown with the real McCoy: someone cracking up in my home.

Compassion plays by different rules when someone psychologically disturbed comes into your life. All the nicey-nicey stuff goes away. They can't interact with you in a linear way, and all the sensible advice in books on communication means nothing when they are screaming or sobbing or flashing anger or threatening to do something dangerously rash, like drive off into the night in a state of mania—or maybe get violent when their pathetic victimhood state runs out of steam. They don't want to be touched. They can't relax. They may or may not do what you tell them. (Boundaries? An insane person smashes right through boundaries.) I had compassion for her when I was trying to help her get through her hurdles on my terms, but when she rejected all my offers of support that also protected me, I just didn't care about her at all. She was clearly going to sabotage any sensible solution to her dilemma and get deeper into her trauma until she ended up being hauled away in a police car. I would have made that call as a last resort.

I had to exorcise this dreadful disturbance from my home. She had to go away to her own fate, and I had to make that happen. The words came to me clearly, "She is disposable." I found my heart of stone—something I thought only other people had. I felt the chill of withdrawing all connection. I understood in an instant how humans can kill each other in inhuman situations. Shooting the hostages. Hit men. War. Executions. Cold-blooded murder. She was a delete button on my emotional keyboard. She was a character I cut out of my script. She was collateral damage to my survival. You have to go away. My cold heart drove her out, even though I made a final offer, kind of a reprieve, for an arrangement with rules and an end date. She didn't want physical security; she wanted me to want her, to care for her, to be her friend. I didn't want her. I had no intention of caring for her. She couldn't be my friend. She was, in fact, my enemy. I locked my house for the first time ever.

There will be more and more people like her on the street and fewer and fewer resources to take care of them as our economic contraction continues. When you say dealing with the bureaucracy drives you crazy, remember that there are more fragile people than you who really will go crazy trying to get help for the basics: shelter, pain relief, safety, human love. The crazier they get, the harder it will be to get those basics. Government programs are stretched to the limit, and spiritual sanctuaries don't want nut cases.

So here we are, in this together, this big fat mess we call society. Because of the warrior life I've led, I can absorb some of the disturbance that is in the air. I'll make a sacrifice to help someone, but now I know I also can sacrifice the person and not look back. It is a strange revelation, finding this capacity to not love. It's added a dimension to the loving part of my life because I am conscious that love is an option. I tell my story because I found out I am not Buddha or Jesus. (And I wish the Fifth Buddha and the Second Coming Jesus would get their butts here and help us out of our mess.) If I run into a psychiatric nurse, I think I'll ask some advice about how to handle a psycho so I'll do better next time. There probably will be a next time, the way things are going.

Raising Rockettes

Sandra Nicholls

THE ROCKETTES were doing it before I was born, the old tap-and-kick routine. I had it down by four. Daddy wanted a Shirley Temple; he was lucky, he had two. Sisters with sausage curls and a will to please, we were dancing with our first steps. Cigarette in one hand, bourbon in the other, he would stand next to the fireplace and announce to assembled guests that two young prima donnas had just arrived straight from Radio City Music Hall in New York and were on hand to entertain them this very evening. Char and I would come running down the hall and burst into the living room in our black-patent tap shoes and pink ruffles, singing and shuffling to "I'm a Yankee Doodle Dandy" or "I'm Looking Over a Four-Leafed Clover," and then jump right into our special rendition of "Be sure it's true when you say I love you, it's a sin to tell a lie."

We took it in stride, believed it was what every girl-child was expected to be able to do, entertain. We had a closet full of costumes and an excuse to wear lipstick and rouge. Dancing lessons were once a week at Betty Merriweather's School of Dance on H Street in Eureka, piano with Miss Wisenfelter, who owned a cat that could open the door. Every day we sang our whole repertoire as soon as we climbed into the back of the Plymouth for a ride across town. Evenings, Daddy romanced the saxophone, cradling it like a baby, swaying around the living room. It wasn't long before Char and I were playing the clarinet and marching in a band. Saturday nights we often went dinner-dancing. Daddy taught us swing, the two-step, and the waltz, giving each of us a turn. Mom was included, but preferred to observe. I never made it to Broadway, but to this day I can't sit still when the band begins to play. I wish we could go around Daddy, just one more time!

The Bounty of the Bioregion

SPONSORED BY GALLERY ROUTE ONE

Art teacher Rose Halady led dozens of students in researching, designing, and painting two 4,000-square-foot murals in the Tomales High School cafeteria in a project initiated and underwritten by Gallery Route One. The subject was the bounty of the local bioregion, from its Miwok past to the present day.

Tomales High School Murals
Painted by Students, 2003 – 2007

Said Rose: "There is magic in creative collaboration. Students learn to meld styles and see their flaws enfolded into the beauty of the larger piece. Big undertakings empower youth. The result gives to the whole community and offers a story that carries forward."

David Geisinger, *The Memory—II—Absence,* 2000, mixed media, 31 x 20 inches

Tomales Bank Robbery, 1996

Blair Fuller

IN 1990 I bought a house on "Maine Street" in Tomales. The house had been built before 1876 and was dilapidated, unpainted for many years and not lived in for ten or fifteen. The family that owned it had put it on the market five years before.

Tomales was then a seen-better-days small town. It had been founded by Irishman John Keys in 1850 when he discovered a usable port up an estuary from Tomales Bay. Ports are rare on the northern California coast, and Keys's small schooner, the *Spray,* could sail north from San Francisco and within two days turn south into Tomales Bay and, with luck, into the estuary hours later. A deep-water tidal pool lay just below the present junction of Route One and the Tomales-Petaluma Road. It made a snug, well-protected harbor.

Keys built a dock, then a warehouse, then a house for himself near the water. He planted potatoes along the creek that emptied into the estuary from the broad, shallow valley to the east, and he soon declared he would provide a passenger and freight service to San Francisco and back.

Doubtless Keys picked up cargo at the Miwok village on nearby Tom's Point and perhaps other villages as well. The few accounts of those years describe an area teeming with fish and game, and the Miwoks were adept at trapping both.

Keys filed a claim for the area surrounding the anchorage and port. Soon a trickle of Anglo farmers and herders began to appear around Tomales's "Lower Town," as it came to be called, to work the surrounding unfenced and unploughed rolling countryside. People were pouring into California from all over the world, and many saw better opportunities than to hunt for gold itself. In a few years Keys could declare that his to and fro voyages would be "weekly."

In 1874 the tracks of the Northwest Pacific Railroad reached the newly built Tomales Station. The trains originated alongside a San Francisco Bay wharf in Sausalito, came north through Fairfax and the San Geronimo Valley to Point Reyes Station, and continued up the east side of Tomales Bay to the town. In the years that followed, track-laying would continue to the north, to Valley Ford, Freestone, then over the mountain and down to Monte Rio on the Russian River, and west along the river to Duncans Mills near the river's mouth at the Pacific.

There were many tiny stations along the railroad's route to which farmers and foresters could bring their freight and for which the trains could be flagged to take on cargoes. Going south, the Northwest Pacific hauled a good percentage of the redwood and Douglas fir that built the city of San Francisco.

The "Upper Town" of Tomales grew up around the railroad station. Its major entrepreneur was Canadian-born Warren Dutton, who was also, it seems, a developer-born. He produced the earliest map of the street grid and became a shop and a hotel owner as the town grew. The Lower Town had faded in importance over the years as the estuary filled in with silt washed down from the potato fields during the rainy seasons, and the building of the railroad bridge over the Walker Creek estuary punctuated the ending of the port's career. (The two stout bridge supports still stand in the middle of the estuary, and vestiges of the railroad's causeways can be seen at many points along Tomales Bay.)

Thus began the period of Tomales's expansion to a population of perhaps no more than 500 permanent residents, but with five hotels, eight saloons, and three automobile dealerships by 1920. Dutton had built himself a suitably substantial house on the west side of Maine Street (now Route One). Up the street from Dutton, on the street's east side, my house had been built for a physician, Dr. Albert Winn. He received patients behind the corner door of his ground-floor office, and his surgery was upstairs, on the second floor.

In 1874, perhaps in response to all those saloons, a local version of the Women's Christian Temperance Union raised the funds to construct the Tomales Town Hall four doors north of the Winn House. Most of the money came from Warren Dutton, a teetotaler. The Town Hall has been in use ever since, renovated and enlarged in 1930 and again in 2008, but with virtually all its original timbers still standing. Since the "great experiment" called Prohibition came to an end in 1932, wine and beer have been served at many weddings and other celebrations in the Hall, with no ghost-caused disasters reported.

Of the eight saloons, only the William Tell revived in 1932. The "Tell" claims to be the oldest saloon in all of Marin County, and is a survivor in a "downtown business district" reduced by catastrophic fires, one of which destroyed the Dutton house and several hotels in 1920. Train service to Tomales ended in 1930 when it fell victim to more flexible truck drayage and the already deepening Great Depression.

My first visit to Tomales was in late 1989. Earlier that year I'd had a quadruple coronary bypass and, recovering, came to feel certain that the entire world was essentially and importantly benign. My first decision in this new phase of life was to buy a boat to sail on Tomales Bay, which to me was the most interesting and beautiful bay imaginable, alive with thousands of birds, fish, harbor seals, and sea lions.

I had not entirely got my strength back when I found a sweet old 21-foot sloop for sale in the Oakland estuary—I was then living in San Francisco, as I had been for many years. I had the boat trucked up to the Marshall Boat Works and dropped into the bay.

Wonderfully satisfying, I was sailing again and it was as pleasing as I had imagined, even if I ran aground on unexpected shallows and had to wait for the incoming tide to lift me off. I did tire out, though, and as I sat waiting for the nudge of the rising water, I began to wonder if I could find a small, cheap house so that I would not have to return to San Francisco at the end of each sailing day.

I looked at houses in Point Reyes Station, Inverness, and Marshall itself, but all that I saw were discouragingly priced, and I reached Tomales with little hope. A Caltrans sign on Route One told me that Tomales's population was 250, but my first impression was that it was even smaller than that. There were no stop signs or traffic lights on the highway or at the single cross street.

I parked near the William Tell and—to my astonishment—a branch of the Bank of America. How could a major American bank make enough profit here to keep a branch open?

There it was, however, a smallish, neo-classical stone façade structure with faux columns framing the glass entry doors and tall, formal-looking windows above. Business hours were listed on the doors, and through the glass I saw an interior like those in the banks that Bonnie and Clyde robbed in the 1930s. To the right was a high partition of opaque glass and dark wood trim, cut into by two small tellers' windows, one of them with an "Open" sign showing. To the left were dark, grim-looking wooden chairs, rigidly arranged, and a single, bare high table. No people were in sight.

Outside at the corner I found a plaque that stated that a bank had been at this location since 1875 but that the present structure had been built in 1920. From that spot I looked across a large, empty lot to Dillon Beach Road running west, and on its far side Diekmann's General Store, "established 1867." In that lonely moment I was grateful to see a Real Estate sign on the east side of Route One, and there I spoke with an agent who seemed pleasantly surprised to see a stranger but who was quickly disappointing. Nothing was for sale in town except a thirteen-acre parcel suitable for grazing livestock. However, as we spoke, I saw through her window a For Sale sign on a very rundown-looking house further up the street and I pointed it out to her.

She conceded that there was such a sign but said that the family that owned the property refused to speak to real estate agents. She lifted her chin, saying that she had no idea what they were asking for, in fact, two old houses side by side and a field in back with a small barn on it. "You'll have to call the owners," she said, clearly saying goodbye to me in the same breath.

Starting back to San Francisco, passing through the rolling, spring-green farmlands between Tomales and Petaluma with broad-shouldered Sonoma Mountain in the distance ahead of me, I was thinking that the chances of finding my imagined house were dim indeed, but that I would call the For Sale phone number, no stone left unturned.

The Sebastiani family was asking $95,000 for the entire property. My friend, architect and former building contractor Greg DeLory, came to Tomales with me to determine whether the structures could be made habitable, and he said yes, they could. *Really?* In spite of *this* and many *that's?* But he held to his opinion.

So I bought the property, together with wrecks of antique vehicles and farm equipment, a water well only thirty feet deep, a concrete front step to the main house imprinted by one of the Sebastiani children's bare feet, and any number of cobwebs.

I was born in New York City and lived there as an adult, too, then in Paris, and in San Francisco for many years—never in a small town. From the novels of Sinclair Lewis I had the idea that it would be essential to patronize local businesses, otherwise I might make no friends and never fit into the community. Who then lived here?

Struck by the number of Italian family names attached to farms and ranches—Cerini, Sartori, Gobbi, Pozzi—I inquired and learned that the "old country" for these families was not Italy itself but the one Italian-speaking canton of Switzerland on the southern face of the Alps. Their migration had taken place gradually from the last years of the nineteenth century into the early years of the twentieth.

(A later series of articles in the weekly *Point Reyes Light* showed that the local Irish had come from small communities in County Galway, the Croatians who settled around the bay from two small Adriatic Islands, the Portuguese from the Azores after a disastrous earthquake in 1907, and the Mexicans from villages near Lake Chapala, east of Guadalajara. In every case there had been an adventurous first person followed by immediate family, relatives, and friends.)

Two of the best-known Tomalans of the Swiss-Italian group were both named Romeo—Romeo or "Rome" Sartori and Romeo or "Butch" Cerini. Rome was locally famous for sometimes driving two hundred and fifty miles or so to have lunch in Reno or South Lake Tahoe in order to test his luck at the blackjack tables before returning home. When he died, a table set up at the entrance to his memorial service at the Town Hall held a photograph of him astraddle his Harley with his fancy cowboy boots one to each side.

Romeo "Butch" Cerini was a less mobile man. A dairy farmer who owned nearly five hundred acres around the Lower Town, he and his wife Gail were childless. Both died within a short time of one another in the early 2000s, and when their joint will was opened, it was learned that Tomales institutions—the Volunteer Fire Department, the Town Hall, the Roman Catholic church, and the Tomales Regional History Center—would all receive substantial sums, and that one million dollars had been left to Tomales High School to help deserving students continue on to college.

My own project to renovate the two old houses and pull upright the barn, which was leaning southward at a radical angle, had its complications. The Tomales Design Review Board did not like my first proposal that would have moved one house to the back lot to make room for parking and a garden off Route One. Both of the houses were said to be essential to the appearance of Maine Street. The second plan was to move the smaller house to the rear of the Maine Street lot, again to make room for a garden and cars.

This was agreed to in Tomales but the county's permit process was slow. Contemporary requirements were often at odds with historic conservation preferences, but after many conferences and adjustments we had a permit.

The lowest bid to do the work came from Bill Bonini Jr. who had spent his entire life in Tomales. His excellent work and Greg DeLory's plans have been much admired—in fact, they won an award from the National Trust for Historic Preservation for restoration of antique buildings.

Before work could be started, however, I went to the Bank of America branch to borrow money. The building appeared to be unchanged in all its details since I had first looked in, including the positioning of the chairs.

I entered, went to the teller's window with the Open sign, and pushed down on the little bell ringer, which chimed loudly.

I heard a man's shoes approaching the far side of the window, then he and I stooped down to see one another through the window's bars, both of us cocking our heads to the right to further diminish our tallness. In this odd position—seeing each other's faces not quite upside down—I introduced myself. I'd bought the Sebastiani house up the street.

"Oh, yes."

"I'm going to need a loan to do the renovation."

"We don't do that sort of a loan."

"Even if I have an account with you?"

"What kind of an account?"

"A checking account."

He paused a moment, then said, "I were you, I'd try the Petaluma office," and his face disappeared upwards.

In 1996 the work on my house had been completed and I had been using it for weekends for some time when this same bank branch made unexpected news.

Three men in a Volkswagen "bug" coming from the south on Route One had driven up and stopped their car directly in front of the bank's glass doors. They pulled ski masks over their heads. Two of them got out of the car and went to the bank's doors while the third remained behind the wheel with the motor running. Witnesses later could not agree as to whether the two men at the doors showed pistols or whether, instead, bulges in their pockets only suggested they were armed.

They pushed on the glass doors and were no doubt surprised to find them unbudgeable, at least until they noticed the sign: "Closed for lunch 12:00 – 12:30."

They knocked, politely at first. Two bank employees inside had, in fact, been interrupted eating, and whether they chose simply to respect the bank's lunch hour rules or whether they had spotted the giveaway ski masks on the men's heads, they hid themselves behind the opaque partition and did not let the robbers in.

The two men attempted to force the door, but the frame and the glass held. Then, realizing that they were stymied, they got quickly back into the "bug" and made their getaway driving north on Route One.

I savored the report of this drama in the *Point Reyes Light.* I read it over many times. The champion bone-headedness of it all! That the robbers had not known the bank would close for lunch! That they should pull on ski masks while still outside! That their getaway car was a Volkswagen "bug," the slowest car commonly seen on American highways!

Despite the many miles they had to travel before they might feel safer in crowded city streets, they remained "at large," and in fact were never apprehended. For their own sakes, as well as the safety of others, I hoped they would never again attempt a bank robbery, or the robbery of anything else.

The incident made me reflect on my own lapses of common sense. Would my luck hold and the gods of navigation forgive my sloop's runnings-aground? On the other hand, might my luck be due to run out?

At this time I was nearing the end of the research I was doing for my book, *Art in the Blood: Seven Generations of American Artists in the Fuller Family,* and it occurred to me that Tomales would be a

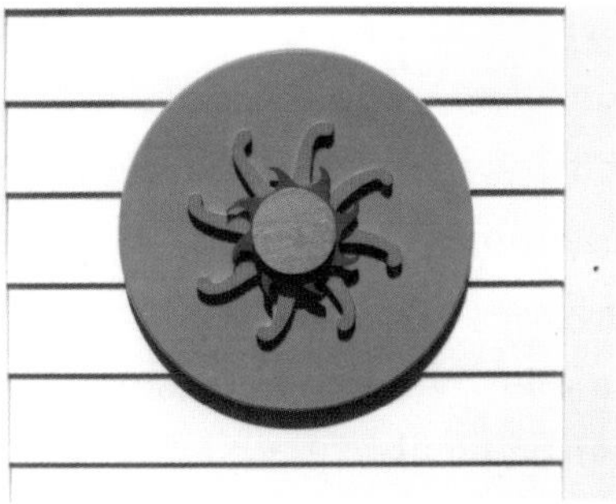

A Victorian sunburst crafted
by Blair Fuller

good place to write it. I would have plenty of space to spread papers around, plenty of quiet and time to brood about both my ancestors and contemporaries in painting and sculpture.

So it came to be. The book was written and published. Since then I've done other written works here, and I've attempted a new kind of work, too. After years of writing and teaching writing I tried my hand at constructing and painting symbolic representations of the sun, either to fit into the gables of houses as "sunbursts" or simply to adorn walls. They were originally Victorian-era "carpenter art"—none of their creators signed their work. When I had first noticed the three examples in the gables of Tomales houses my coronary bypass was fresh in mind, and I treasured what I took to be the impulse that produced the "sunbursts"—an expression of joy in the sun and a generous wish to beam a reminder of its rays to all who passed by.

People die, and their houses pass into new hands. Also, real estate boomed in Tomales and some residents took advantage of the rise in prices to sell and to move northward or eastward. New people turned up from the city to find "second homes." There have not been many new people—the total number of houses in Tomales has scarcely changed, and until quite recently, I would have said that the feeling of the town has remained pretty constant.

On the bakery's outdoor benches a San Francisco cardiologist who rides a Ducati may be sitting with a local cabinet maker, or a man who repairs bagpipes, a woman who teaches school, or the retired Creative Director of the Intel Corporation. They will be served by Cameron, the owner, who was once the pastry chef in a many-starred San Francisco hotel and who takes her scuba-diving vacations in such places as Bali, and by a beautiful young woman who raises rescued snakes.

At the Tell an adventurous Englishwoman who is now the owner of the town's Continental Inn may be sitting on a barstool with a dairyman or a small-scale theatrical entrepreneur or a foundations and paving contractor at either side. She is often joined by a woman friend who works part-time for Caltrans. Five-dollar hamburgers every Monday night. TV with ball games on.

Nearly two years ago, however, a cottage across the street from me was sold to a lovely woman who is now my wife. I had been single for twenty-three years, she for many years, too. Now she lives in my house—I mean our house, of course. Her career is in the administration of all-girl private schools. She has been Head for long periods of two very successful ones.

The entire town has become better looking. There are more flowers blooming, there is more fresh paint on the houses. Or is it that, in the words of Lorenz Hart, "She can make me believe it's a beautiful world."

Witness

David Swain

I have no wish to become
a collector of feathers and bones
but the evidence accumulates:
beneath the eucalyptus a pair
of excised woodpecker wings,
the husk of a mantis
in mid-supplication,
a waning iridescence
punctuating the fence-wire—
suspended in stillness
a solitary hummingbird intent
on thrill or escape, flouting
its delicate filament of neck,
breeze burnishing the gorget's flame.
So even these creatures are fallible.

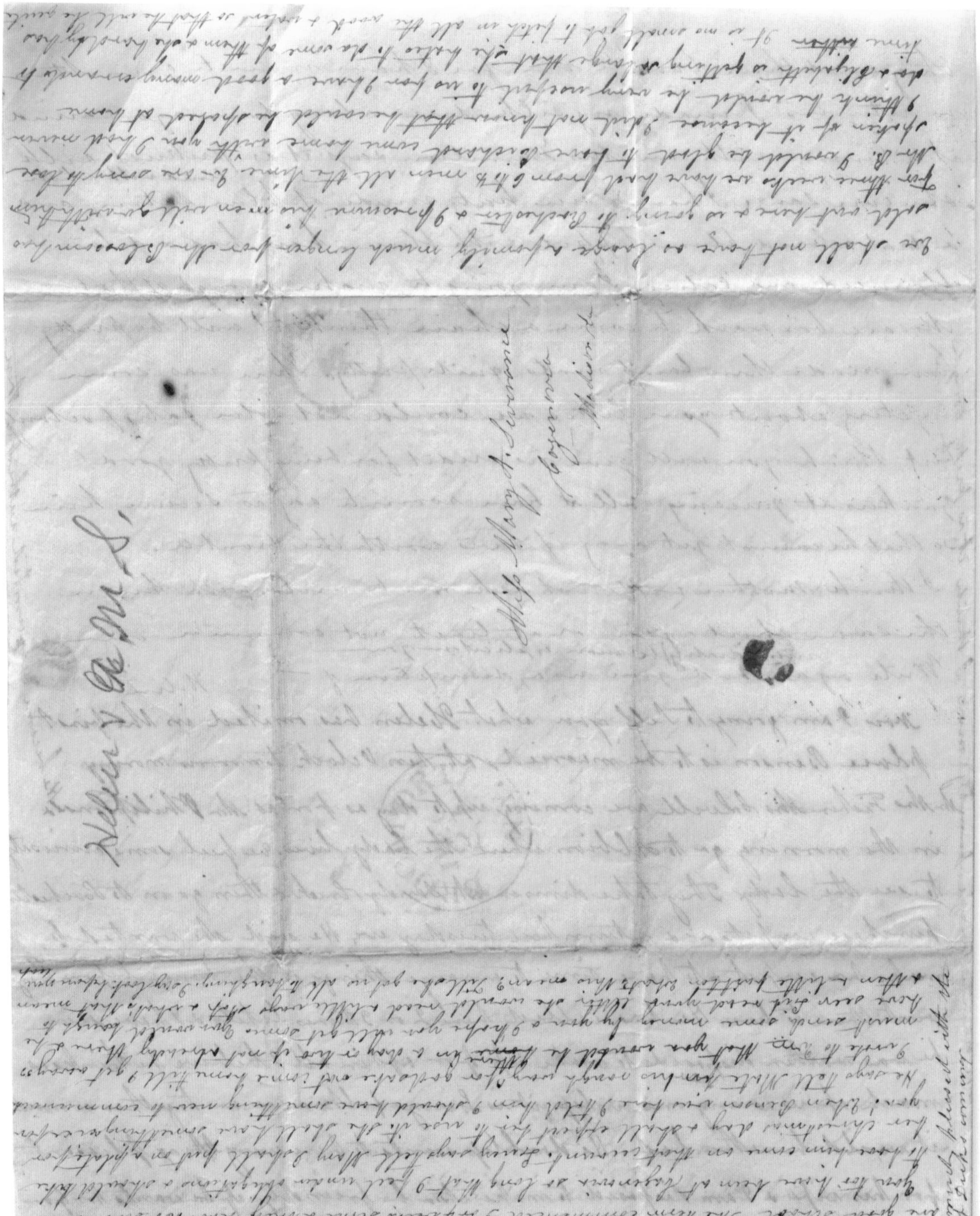

The folds and small remnant of red sealing wax provide evidence this undated letter was written before the Civil War, when mail was weighed and hand posted without envelopes or stamps. A walk or buggy ride to the post office was an opportunity, much as it is today in West Marin, to meet, share gossip, and exchange news about what was going on in town.

Belles Lettres

Notes on Penmanship and Cross-Writing by Carola DeRooy

FROM THE WATT COLLECTION OF SHAFTER FAMILY PAPERS
COURTESY OF THE JACK MASON MUSEUM OF WEST MARIN HISTORY, INVERNESS
ARTIFACT PHOTOGRAPHY BY THOMAS HEINSER

Shafter Family in Olema, 1895: (left to right) Payne and Helen Shafter, Mary Severence Jackson, Dr. James Shafter, Emma Shafter Howard, Julia Shafter Hamilton. Front row, Helen and Mary Shafter.

THE PLEASURE of leafing through 19th-century letters comes from the feel of the paper, the undulations of ink, and imagining you can decipher something about the writers through the characteristics of their unique script. In the age of pen and ink, one began to master script as a youth, practicing in a diary, like Mary Severence, who began hers at age nine. Advanced practitioners corresponded using a fine hand and cryptic cross-writing. When Mary's daughter, Helen, married into the Shafter family—owners of the majority of land on the Point Reyes Peninsula from 1850 to1930—it was a merger of two dynastic and prolific letter-writing families. To read between the lines of the mundane and extraordinary events of their lives is to know them better and to appreciate the art of practiced penmanship.

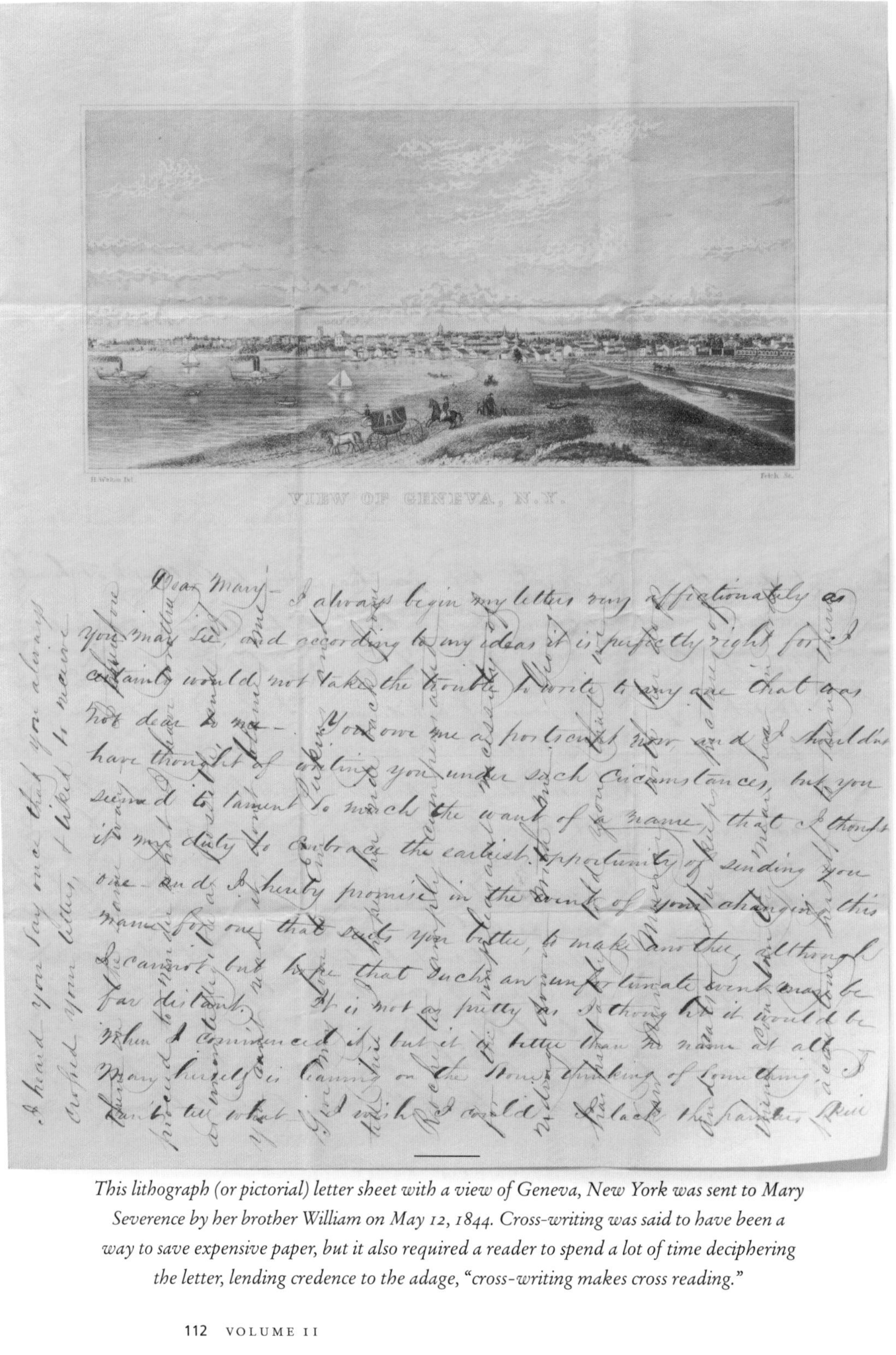
VIEW OF GENEVA, N.Y.

Dear Mary— I always begin my letters very affectionately as you may see, and according to my ideas it is perfectly right for I certainly would not take the trouble to write to any one that was not dear to me— You owe me a portrait now, and I shouldn't have thought of writing you under such circumstances, but you seemed to lament so much the want of a name, that I thought it my duty to embrace the earliest opportunity of sending you one and I hereby promise in the event of your changing this name for one that suits you better, to make another, although I cannot but hope that such an unfortunate event may be far distant. It is not as pretty as I thought it would be when I commenced it, but it is better than no name at all. Mary herself is leaning on the stone thinking of something, I can't tell what— I wish I could—

I heard you say once that you always prized your letters, & liked to receive

This lithograph (or pictorial) letter sheet with a view of Geneva, New York was sent to Mary Severence by her brother William on May 12, 1844. Cross-writing was said to have been a way to save expensive paper, but it also required a reader to spend a lot of time deciphering the letter, lending credence to the adage, "cross-writing makes cross reading."

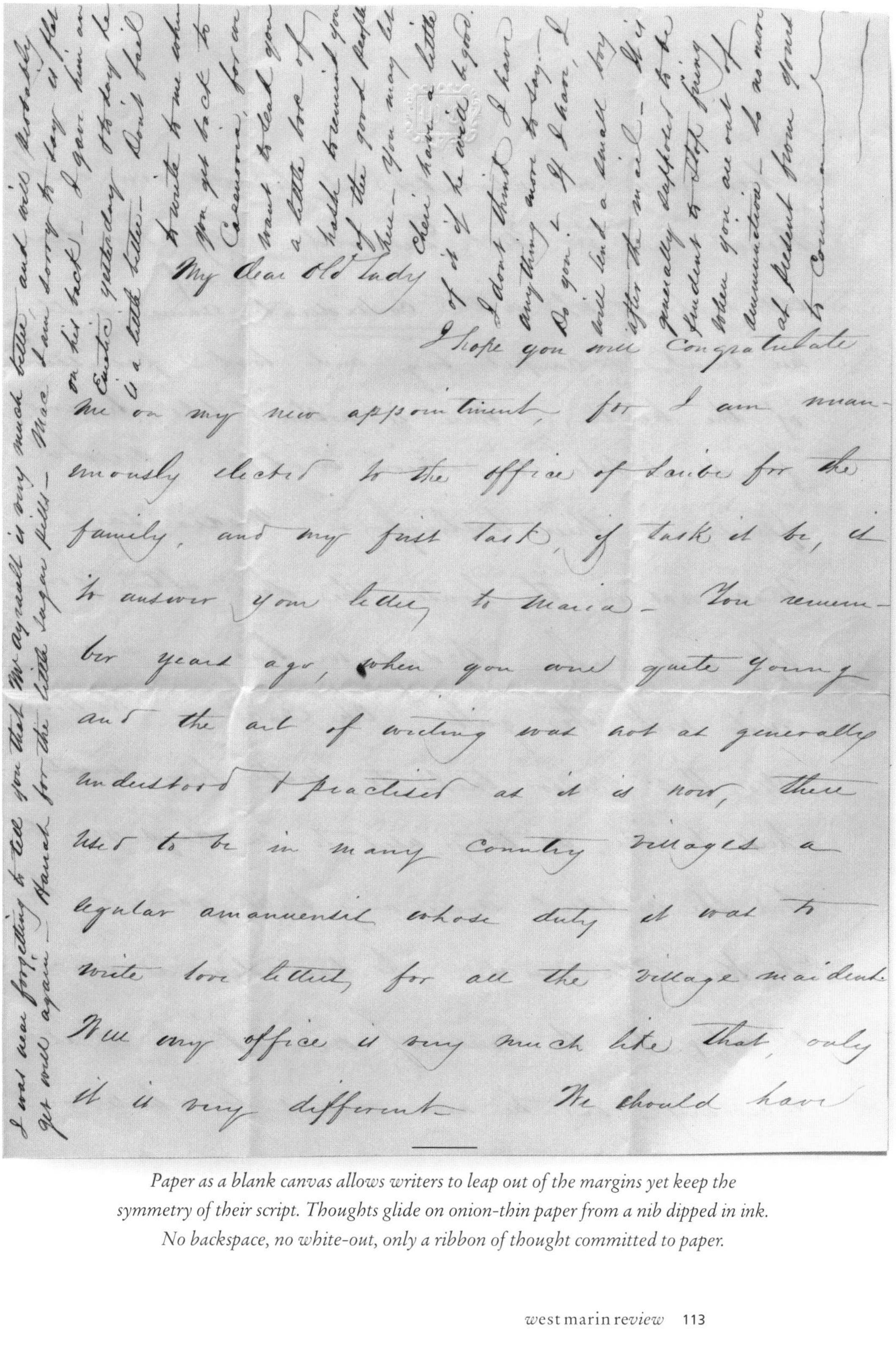
My Dear Old Lady

I hope you will congratulate me on my new appointment, for I am unanimously elected to the office of Scribe for the family, and my first task, if task it be, is to answer your letter to Maria — You remember years ago, when you were quite young and the art of writing was not as generally understood & practised as it is now, there used to be in many country villages a regular amanuensis whose duty it was to write love letters for all the village maidens. Well my office is very much like that, only it is very different — We should have

Paper as a blank canvas allows writers to leap out of the margins yet keep the symmetry of their script. Thoughts glide on onion-thin paper from a nib dipped in ink. No backspace, no white-out, only a ribbon of thought committed to paper.

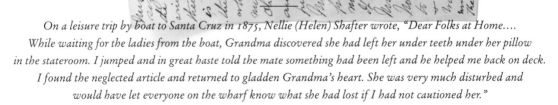

On a leisure trip by boat to Santa Cruz in 1875, Nellie (Helen) Shafter wrote, "Dear Folks at Home.... While waiting for the ladies from the boat, Grandma discovered she had left her under teeth under her pillow in the stateroom. I jumped and in great haste told the mate something had been left and he helped me back on deck. I found the neglected article and returned to gladden Grandma's heart. She was very much disturbed and would have let everyone on the wharf know what she had lost if I had not cautioned her."

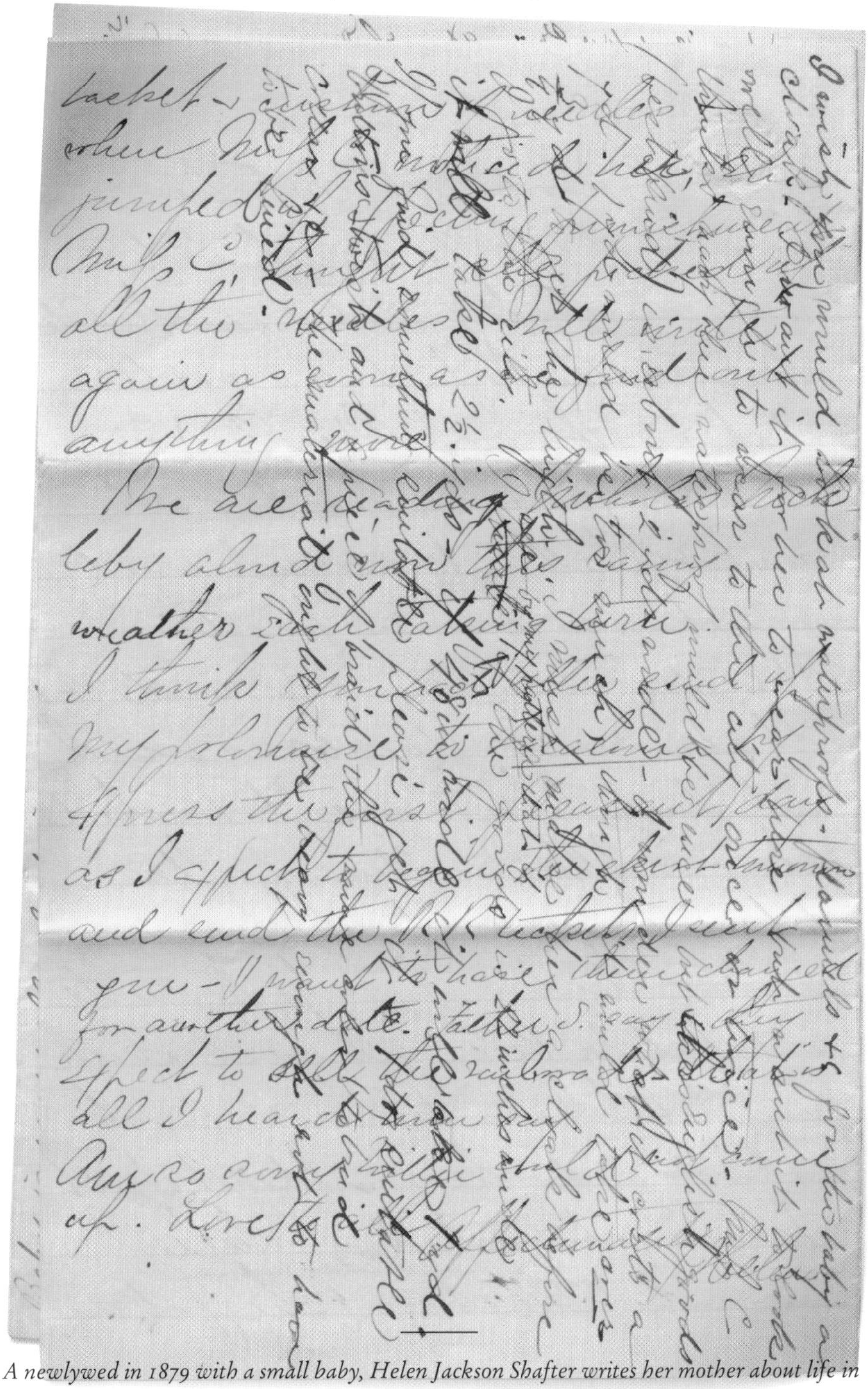

A newlywed in 1879 with a small baby, Helen Jackson Shafter writes her mother about life in the country house in Olema, including the roof leaking after a storm, the baby crying, and missing her husband, who was several days away by horseback. In the cross-written section, Helen describes in detail all the yardage measurements and fabric she would like for sewing new clothes, confident that her mother, who taught her the technique, will decipher the details.

The Last Bison Gone

Rebecca Foust

Ours is the curse of the blighted touch
that wilts every green shoot and flower
we mean to admire, keep, re-create

or improve. New Zealand's Huia Bird,
prized for her scimitar beak
and pleated Victorian petticoat tail,

was hunted extinct except for this
diving-belled brooch and sad hatband,
fast falling to dust

in the Smithsonian. We love what we love
in the scientific way, efficient, empiric,
vicious, too much

and always we touch it, our breath
blooming algae on the walls of Lascaux,
shimmering in acid-etch green.

Song of the Field

Murray Silverstein

The song of the field is the buzz of the mind
          of the man in the field.
To enter the mind, enter the field

but the song in the mind is the hum of the woods
          at the edge of the field
& to enter the edge, you must enter the woods

but the song of the woods is the caw of the crow
          at the top of the pine
& to enter the woods, you must enter the crow.

Dear Friends in Minnesota

Agnes Wolohan Smuda von Burkleo

Tonight, in northern California,
in this sudden heat wave,
we sit on the back porch as if
it were summer in the Midwest.
The heat brings you close,
the sound of distant voices down the creek,
gentle voices, as if a baby were asleep,
shy to be speaking in such beauty in the dark.
Later, the long white sheets drape our bodies.
Fan breezes sweep our skin like searchlight.
The slow breathing of the thick night holds us still,
just as the trees are held, their leaves relaxing utterly.
You are with us in this hush, across time zones
and in translations of language born of landscapes:
"kelp" for me, 10:00 p.m., perhaps "rhubarb" for you, midnight.
The same sun that popped out of the prairie's pocket,
lingered, liquid gold
on the ocean's dark blue belly,
then dropped like a coin into a purse,
currency of friendship.

An, Ode, to Coffee,

Come to me Hebe, maiden divine,
Bring me my coffee tis better than wine
Bring it all steaming, so I may sip,
From out of the cup that has touched thy lips,
Bring it all steaming rich with perfume,
Scenting the air, and filling the room,
We,ll, sit together by morning light,
Drinking our coffee breakfast delight,
You drink from my cup. I,ll drink from thine,
In changing the cups, I find your hand in mine,
Give me one rose, from your cheeks so fair,
nd I of my Tulips will give you a pair,
ome to me Hebe, maiden divine
ring me my coffee, tis better than wine,

P. J. S.

Payne Jewett Shafter, *An Ode to Coffee,* circa 1880. Courtesy of the Jack Mason Museum. In Greek mythology, Hebe is the goddess of youth and the cupbearer for the gods and goddesses of Mount Olympus. Perhaps Shafter was inspired when he awoke at dawn on his Olema estate, The Oaks (now the Vedanta Retreat), to a cup of steaming coffee, misty morning valley fog, chattering birds, and a muse. —*Carola DeRooy, Archivist*

MOORE
MAP TACKS
100 #103 WHITE
MOORE PUSH-PIN COMPANY

Unpublished Manuscripts

Philip L. Fradkin

EVERY ONCE in a while I go rummaging through my past in an attempt to figure out who I am. Among the various items I recently came across was a newspaper clipping from the December 15, 1932 edition of the *New York Herald Tribune.* The headline over the one-column story that ran on an inside page was "Fiery Cross On Jersey Lawn of Clubwoman." The "clubwoman" was my mother, Elvira Fradkin. Also among the items was an unpublished manuscript of 43,000 words.

These two artifacts encapsulated what I inherited from my mother: an attraction to causes and to the written word. Her activism dated back to her years at Vassar College when she was suspended for a short time for attending a suffragette rally and conference in New York City. It was an exciting time for committed women. British women had stormed Parliament, and American women were marching on Wall Street. There were two large rallies in Carnegie Hall in the last week of October 1909. No silly college rule kept my mother from attending them.

The 1932 newspaper story concerned the burning of a cross on the lawn of my parents' Montclair home by the Ku Klux Klan. The anonymous reporter wrote, "Dr. Fradkin, a Russian-born dentist, apparently is not a target of the demonstration except as the husband of Mrs. Fradkin, the former Elvira Kush, one of the foremost supporters of peace movements, to which the anonymous messages alluded."

H.D. Mott, *Shadowbox,* 2007, mixed media,
21 x 9 3/4 x 1 1/2 inches

The messages, consisting of two letters and a postcard delivered prior to the burning of the cross, read in part: "This is a challenge to the peace movement" and "Challenge to Communism." All were signed "K.K.K." and crosses were drawn on them in red ink. My mother was quoted: "To deliberately confuse the work for peaceful settlements of disputes between nations with Communism is one of the most insidious methods of the Ku Klux Klan to frustrate the efforts for peace."

As for the clubwoman label, the story identified her as president, honorary president, or former chairman of a number of organizations dedicated to international understanding and peace. True, listed among the groups were womens' clubs and those oriented toward women university graduates, my mother having received a master's degree from Columbia University in 1914. The article noted that she had attended the 1932 World Disarmament Conference in Geneva, where she represented fourteen women's groups.

There was an important omission in the background information. My mother also happened to be a published author. A monograph that she had written, titled, *Chemical Warfare: Its Possibilities and Probabilities,* was published by the Carnegie Endowment for International Peace in 1929. It was praised by the president of Columbia as "the most complete work on that subject ever written."

Elvie, as she was known to friends, wrote other articles and gained a following in her field. She spent time in Geneva with a young CBS radio correspondent, Shelby Cullom Davis, and his wife. Forty years later, Davis, then U.S. ambassador to Switzerland, wrote to my sister that my mother's publications "were well known and studied at the time."

Yet she was still a clubwoman to the *Herald Tribune.* I can understand what went on in that newsroom, having worked in such male-dominated places long ago. A stringer dictated the story to a rewrite man, and the headline with the offensive label was attached on the copy desk. In those days "clubwoman" was code for an active, intelligent woman. Two years after the cross-burning incident, which did not deter my mother in the least, her first book, *The Air Menace and the Answer,* was published by Macmillan. She clearly was trespassing in male territory with a powerful totem, a book about warfare. Hoffman Nickerson, the author of another book on weapons and peace, reviewed her book in *The New York Times Book Review.* He wrote, "If anyone wants to know why American pacifists, especially women pacifists, have accomplished so little, the harsh lesson can be learned by cataloging her fallacies."

A number of distinguished people rode to my mother's defense, and there was a spirited exchange of letters in two subsequent issues of the *Book Review.* Among those who wrote was Carrie Chapman Catt, who had led the fight for passage of the constitutional amendment giving women the right to vote and had then turned her formidable energies to the cause of peace. She said the review "sounded as though inspired by a spirit of hostility or an angry militaristic mind." Nickerson wrote a snide reply to his critics and called the book "valueless." My mother marshaled the positive appraisals of others, ranging from the president of the World Organization of Jewish Women to the president of Vassar.

Her third major work, *A World Airlift,* was published by Funk & Wagnalls in 1950. In it my mother advocated a United Nations Air Police Patrol (UNAPP) that would enforce peace. Her friend Eleanor Roosevelt plugged the book in her newspaper column, and my mother appeared on Roosevelt's radio show.

I vividly recall Mrs. Roosevelt's visits to our home at this time. She always knew the right questions to ask a teenager, and she always went into the kitchen to talk with the Negro help. I also remember the football coach in that Republican town calling me "Mrs. Roosevelt" every time I missed a tackle, and the next door neighbor, a stockbroker, becoming choleric about the Roosevelts whenever I entered his house on an errand.

My mother dedicated *A World Airlift* to her family, but we really weren't very supportive. Each member of the family had their own interests, and there was no traditional mother to bind us all together. My father was more interested in his dentistry, I was occupied by sports and girls, and my sister was elsewhere pursuing an acting career. My mother harangued two pairs of closed ears about world peace at the dinner table.

Her last work, an unpublished manuscript, expanded on the idea of an airborne United Nations peace presence and was to have been the capstone of her career. I can still hear my mother say after meeting with editors during a long day in New York, or upon receiving another rejection letter in the mail: "If I only was a man!" I am now an author and get similar letters, but I have never been able to attribute them to my sex. She, unfortunately, was a woman who lived prior to the 1970s and could never reconcile her family and her career.

My mother worked for twenty years on this book and only gave up upon her death in 1972. She was in her eighties. While she labored on the book, I was in Vietnam as a newspaper correspondent witnessing firsthand the questionable effects of air power in that United Nations effort. She was worried about my safety and supportive of my work.

I have never read any of her works. But I did skim part of the unpublished manuscript the other day and saw that she had taken a swipe at her unappreciative family. She cited "the constant rejections both of the basic plan, which I tried out on family, friends, diplomats at the UN, and the so-called experts in arms control. The more rejections, the more I determined to continue."

I salute her determination. I, too, have an unpublished manuscript. The only way there is a chance it might be published is if I persist. When asked by younger writers or students about rejections, I cite my writing mantra, derived from my mother's and my experiences—although she expressed it more politely: "Don't let the bastards get you down."

Igor Sazevich, *Point Reyes Morning Spaces*, 2008, pen-and-ink drawing, 7 1/2 x 5 inches

Writers and Artists

FRANCINE ALLEN was born in San Francisco, moved to Inverness in 1976 and, a miniaturist by nature, has traveled widely in West Marin.

JOHN ANDERSON has been a painter for more than fifty years. In 1955 he dropped out of the University of Illinois and dedicated his life to painting. In 1958 he met his mentor, Gordon Onslow Ford, and moved to Inverness, California.

DONALD BACON retired from teaching English and American literature at Harvard and Stanford. The poem "Oblique Tide" represents a view of Tomales Bay from the ranch where he and his wife and two children spend part of their time.

ROSALEEN BERTOLINO's fiction has recently appeared in *Dark Sky, Stringtown, Marginalia,* and *Tertulia* magazines, as well as the anthology, *The Wandering Mother.* Currently at work on her second novel, she lives in Fairfax, California.

FARIBA BOGZARAN, PhD, studied painting at Exeter college, England and printmaking at the University of Wisconsin. An award-winning artist, she has been a professor at the Department of Arts and Consciousness at JFK University for 18 years and co-founded Lucid Art Foundation, Inverness, California.

AGNES WOLOHAN SMUDA VON BURKLEO grew up during summers in Inverness and dreamt of being a writer, but first she became a musician. She was named a Minnesota Artist of the Year in 2007 for the CD, *Songstories.*

ANGELICA CASEY was a student at Tomales High School in Rachel Somerville's Art One class in 2008.

CLAUDIA CHAPLINE, an international artist/writer, has lived in Stinson Beach since 1987. Her gallery in Stinson Beach is a showcase for West Marin artists. Water is an ongoing theme of her work.

RICH CLARKE lives in Marshall. Born and raised in Berkeley, he has been photographing the beauty, texture, and natural relationships of West Marin since the '60s.

For 17 years, CAROLA DEROOY has used letters, old photos, documents, and maps to illuminate bits of local history. She is the co-author of *Point Reyes Peninsula,* an historical photo book of the area.

A native of San Diego county, BILL DEWEY has been photographing the California landscape from the air and ground for more than 25 years. He attended U.C. Davis, U.C. Santa Barbara, Brooks Institute of Photography, and Rochester Institute of Photography.

Inverness photographer EVVY EISEN's portraits of Holocaust survivors are included in museum collections, a traveling exhibition, and her film, *Multiply by Six Million.* She is photographing Drakes Bay oyster workers to help put a face on this little-known group.

REBECCA FOUST won the 2007 and 2008 Robert Phillips Poetry Chapbook Prize. Nominated for two 2008 Pushcart Prize, her recent poetry appears or is forthcoming in *Atlanta Review, Nimrod, North American Review, Spoon River, Women's Review of Books,* and elsewhere.

PHILIP L. FRADKIN grew up in New Jersey and has spent the last 30 years in West Marin, moving several times back and forth across the San Andreas Fault. He has written 11 books on Alaska and the American West.

Tomales resident BLAIR FULLER wrote the novels, *A Far Place* and *Zebina's Mountain;* a collection of short fiction, *A Butterfly Net and a Kingdom;* and the non-fiction work, *Art in the Blood.* He has taught at Stanford and other universities.

GALLERY ROUTE ONE is a nonprofit, community-based and artist-run organization that presents exhibitions and a supporting educational program serving the cultural, political, and environmental concerns of West Marin and the greater Bay Area. GRO initiated and underwrote the Tomales High School Mural project and the Marin Literacy Photography Project featured in this volume.

MARILYN LONGINOTTI GEARY is an oral historian, writer, and fiber artist who lives in Woodacre, California. She is author of *Marin City Memories,* stories of African Americans who migrated to Marin to work in the shipyards during World War II.

A practicing psychotherapist in San Francisco for more than 40 years, Mill Valley resident DAVID GEISINGER has been painting and doing assemblages for much of that time. Self-taught, he has had several one-man shows in the Bay Area.

KATHLEEN GOODWIN paints, photographs, and publishes from her ridgetop studio on Drakes View Drive in Inverness Park. She also paints on location using water colors, oils, and pastels. She is represented by the Point Reyes Visions Gallery in Inverness Park.

Student artist KYLE GOVAN enjoys living in the country and viewing the land. He enjoys making art "because it is relaxing."

KAREN GRAY and her carpenter husband made their home in the Old Point Reyes Schoolhouse compound thirty years ago, raising children, growing vegetables, tending chickens. Today Karen gardens, hosts nature lovers, and pursues naturalist writing and illustrating.

Kyle Govan, *Untitled,* 2008, mixed media collage on masonite, 7 x 7 inches

BARBARA HEENAN is a senior researcher at Inverness Research, where she spends most of her time writing formal research reports. In recent years, with the encouragement of a handful of friends, she has started writing poetry and personal essays.

STEVE HEILIG is an editor, ethicist, environmentalist, epidemiologist, educator, ethnomusicologist, and author of nonfiction, poetry, criticism, and scientific pieces. He sometimes edits the *Hearsay News* in a coastal village that cannot be named even here.

Photographer THOMAS HEINSER's editorial and advertising images are internationally recognized and are noted for their use of natural light and graphic compositions. www.thomasheinser.com

ANNET HELD is an award-winning photojournalist born and raised in the north of Holland and now living in Paris. She has spent summers in West Marin for 30 years.

ASHLEY HOWZE was a student at Tomales High in Rachel Somerville's Art One class in 2008.

WILLIAM KEENER is an environmental lawyer living in Marin County. His collection of nature poems, *Gold Leaf on Granite,* will be published in 2009 by Anabiosis Press. In 2005 he was awarded an Individual Artist's Grant from the Marin Arts Council.

ELISE KROEBER's photography ranges from ethnographic studies in Guatemala to coverage of strike actions in the Bay Area. She began with black-and-white film, processing her own work. Her images are now digital. She lives in Mill Valley.

KURT LAI reports that he spends too much time resting on benches in West Marin. He says it's where he wants to be when he grows up.

JONATHAN (JON) LANGDON was born in San Francisco in 1938. From there it was UC Berkeley '65, four years Navy, twice married, two kids, boatwright, furniture designer/maker, carpenter, contractor, retired, single but attached, painter, some poetry writing. Mostly happy and content.

ELIZABETH LEAHY has worked on a shrimp boat, an iris ranch, in a kitchen making desserts with a blow torch, and as first copy chief of *Wired* magazine. She swam the English Channel at 40 and is a firefighter in San Francisco.

BARBARA LOVEJOY lives with her three cats on Mt. Tam, where she thrives on nature's wild beauty. The inspiration for the poem "Fog" came one night while she was driving through dense fog on Panoramic Highway.

At age 73, EUGENIA LOYSTER came to Point Reyes Station from Madison, Wisconsin. Her Berkeley daughter, Sara, suggested she write a poem every week so she could join a writers' workshop. The included poem is one of Eugenia's "weeklies."

Student artist MARGARITO LOZA works around cows. He milks cows, cleans their pens, clips their horns, feeds them, and rounds them up. He enjoys making art in art class because it allows him to express himself.

RICK LYTTLE: Although they started vacationing in West Marin in the late '40s, Rick and Jean did not settle here permanently with their family until 1962, she to teach and he to write. Later, he also made a niche as an artist.

Born in Chico, California, student artist RAUL MACIAS lives and works on a local family dairy, where he enjoys the clean air and beach views. He likes making art because it helps him express his emotions in a positive way.

LOUISE MALOOF took a BFA in painting and sculpture at Otis Parsons. A post-structuralist, she uses forms of nature as metaphors for our souls. Her work is collected around the world; her studio is at Hamilton Field Marin Museum of Contemporary Art (MOCA).

MOLLY MARCUSSEN lives on a dairy near Tomales and is a sophomore at Tomales High School. She is a member of the Tomales Future Farmers of America Club and enjoys showing dairy and swine at local fairs.

A third-generation San Franciscan, GALE S. MCKEE was raised in Marin County. She received a BFA from the University of Denver and has worked in Chicago and San Francisco as an art director, graphic designer, and illustrator.

HANNAH (H.D.) MOTT lives on the Inverness Ridge. Her work, "Shadowbox," was inspired by family ephemera found when closing down the family home.

SANDRA NICHOLLS, a former teacher and innkeeper, lives in an ancient house in Valley Ford beside the Estero Americano, where willows stream and the green heron hides.

Raul Macias, *Untitled,* 2008, mixed media collage on masonite, 7 x 7 inches

LINDA PASTAN's *Queen of a Rainy Country* (Norton, 2006) is her twelfth book of poems. She was Poet Laureate of Maryland 1991–1995 and twice a finalist for the National Book Award. In 2003 she won the Ruth Lilly Poetry Prize.

IGOR SAZEVICH lives and paints in West Marin. Sometimes, while taking his ritual coffee at either the Bovine or Toby's, he flips open his sketch book and records the action.

MURRAY SILVERSTEIN's first collection of poems, *Any Old Wolf* (Sixteen Rivers Press), received the Independent Publisher's Award for poetry in 2007. An architect and coauthor of *A Pattern Language* (Oxford University Press), Silverstein lives in Oakland, California.

C. R. SNYDER has been a photographer for 40 years and is a member of Gallery Route One. His work has been published in *Beat Times* and *Photo Metro* and shown in galleries across the United States.

RACHEL SOMERVILLE teaches art at Tomales High School. She recently completed a Master's degree in Art Education at Arizona State University.

NANCY STEIN has painted, gardened, and lived on Inverness ridge for 35 years, inspired by the wild northern California sea.

NELL SULLIVAN is a retired English professor who lives in a four-generation household in West Marin. She has published a textbook on writing, short prose fiction, and many poems. She is presently completing a novel.

DAVID SWAIN was born in Ohio, grew up near Boston, and lives in San Rafael with his wife, Linda, and two sons, Daniel and William.

GARY THORP's most recent book is *Caught in Fading Light,* a study of mountain lions in Marin County. He regularly surveys Point Reyes beaches as part of the Beach Watch program.

Margarito Loza, *Untitled,* 2008, mixed media collage on masonite, 7 x 7 inches

AMANDA TOMLIN shoots medium- and large-format film with mostly vintage cameras and prints in her home darkroom. She is fascinated by how light changes at night and what happens visually when no one is around.

ANNE VITALE, PhD, is a psychotherapist specializing in gender identity issues. She is also the author/editor of an educational Web site, paints still lifes, and goes fly fishing every chance she gets. She lives in Inverness Park.

ELIZABETH WHITNEY is a lifelong journalist and longtime columnist, most recently for the *Malibu Surfside News* (*Making Waves* 2001–2005). She is now home where she belongs in West Marin working on a book project: *Living Well in a Dying Age.*

TERRY TEMPEST WILLIAMS is a naturalist and prolific author of environmental literature, most notably *Refuge: An Unnatural History of Family and Place.* Her poem in this issue is the dramatic opening of her latest book, *Finding Beauty in a Broken World.* She lives in Castle Valley, Utah and Moose, Wyoming.

LAUREL WROTEN lives in Marshall. Between freezer runs, she is working on a collection of vignettes about life in West Marin. Laurel is a former advertising copywriter. For a time, she also contributed regularly to *A Prairie Home Companion.*

Connections

WRITING ORGANIZATIONS/EDUCATION

Marin Arts Council, Poet Laureate Program
www.marinarts.org

Marin Poetry Center
www.marinpoetrycenter.org

Mesa Refuge Writers Retreat
www.commoncounsel.org

River of Words
www.riverofwords.org

Tomales Bay Library Association
www.co.marin.ca.us/library/wmarin/tbla.cfm

Tomales Bay Writers' Conference
At the Marconi Center
www.extension.ucdavis.edu

VISUAL ARTS

Bolinas Museum
www.bolinasmuseum.org

Claudia Chapline Contemporary Art
www.cchapline.com

Gallery Route One
www.galleryrouteone.org

Falkirk Cultural Center
www.falkirkculturalcenter.org

Toby's Gallery
www.tobysfeedbarn.com

EVENTS

Dance Palace Community Center
www.dancepalace.org

Marin Events
www.marinevents.com

Point Reyes Books
www.ptreyesbooks.com

San Geronimo Valley Community Center
www.sgvcc.org

AGRICULTURE + LAND STEWARDSHIP

Environmental Forum of Marin
www.marinefm.org

Marin Agricultural Land Trust
www.malt.org

Marin Organic
www.marinorganic.org

Marin Resource Conservation District
www.marinrcd.org

UC Agriculture and Natural Resources
www.growninmarin.org
cemarin.ucdavis.edu

ENVIRONMENT + WILDERNESS

Audubon Canyon Ranch
www.egret.org

Point Reyes National Seashore
www.nps.gov/pore

Point Reyes National Seashore Association
www.ptreyes.org

Environmental Action Committee
of West Marin
www.eacmarin.org

Occidental Arts and Ecology Center
www.oaec.org

Regenerative Design Institute
www.regenerativedesign.org

Tomales Bay Watershed Council
www.tomalesbaywatershed.org

NEWS + INFORMATION

KWMR Community Radio
www.kwmr.org

West Marin Citizen
www.westmarincitizen.com

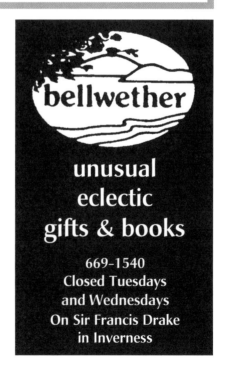

THE BOY WHO WOULD BE TSAR

by ANDREW ROMANOFF

Andrew's memoirs of growing up on the grounds of Windsor Castle, England, together with his art done in shrinky dink. *Published by Griff Williams, Urban Digital Color (Gallery 16), San Francisco, CA.*

To order a signed copy, contact
POINT REYES BOOKS
T: 415.663.1542
BOOKS@PTREYESBOOKS.COM
WWW.PTREYESBOOKS.COM

G•R•O

GALLERY ROUTE ONE

A NON-PROFIT ARTIST-RUN GALLERY

25 *Years of great art, community outreach and involvement with environmental projects and Artists in the Schools.*

11101 Highway One, Pt. Reyes Station
Open daily: 11 am–5 pm
Closed: Tuesdays
415 663-1347
www.galleryrouteone.org

POINT REYES NATION
SERVING THE WEST MARIN COMMUNITY

In service to the West Marin Community and its Non Profits

FREE & CLEAR

Sponsors of "FREE & CLEAR" Water for West Marin and the West Marin Community Event Library

Information at pointreyesnation.com

KWMR

90.5 FM PT. REYES | **89.9 FM BOLINAS**

WEST MARIN COMMUNITY RADIO

KWMR is non-commercial community radio offering a wide range of information and entertainment from our studios in the Creamery Building, downtown Point Reyes Station.

www.kwmr.org

West Marin Citizen
Speaking the language of West Marin
Citizen
Commission signs off on landfill plan
HOME DELIVERY!
Community Newspaper
Published Every Thursday
CATCH THE WEEKLY NEWS. Call 415-723-6948 or 415-663-8232
Online at www.westmarincitizen.com

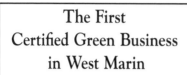

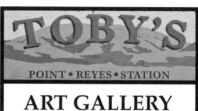

About the West Marin Review

West Marin Review
Volume II, Summer 2009

ISBN 978-0-9822829-1-5

The *West Marin Review* is a publishing collaboration among Tomales Bay Library Association, Point Reyes Books, and Steering Committee Members David Miller, Steve Costa, Nancy Adess, Madeleine Corson, Ellen Serber, and Doris Ober.

A special thanks for help organizing events and distribution to Nancy Kelly, Jody Farrell, Ellen Serber, Judith Shaw, and Chris Gruener, and to Elisabeth Ptak and Sandy Duveen for excellent proofreading.

Published by the Tomales Bay Library Association, Post Office Box 984, Point Reyes Station, CA 94956
www.westmarinreview.org

FRONT COVER PHOTO William B. Dewey, *Bay Patterns #2,* (entrance to Drakes Bay, Point Reyes National Seashore) 2005

BACK COVER Annet Held, *Jan Schreur, Boatbuilder in Giethoorm,* circa 1950

SUBMISSIONS FOR VOLUME III
Submissions guidelines: www.westmarinreview.org or info@westmarinreview.org. Submissions accepted year-round, only by mail. Mail submissions to: West Marin Review c/o Tomales Bay Library Association, Post Office Box 984, Point Reyes Station, CA 94956

SUPPORT THE *WEST MARIN REVIEW!*
The *West Marin Review* is created through the volunteer efforts of friends, neighbors, artists, and writers. Donations are appreciated (and tax-deductible!). Please make checks payable to the Tomales Bay Library Association and note *West Marin Review* on the memo line. You are also invited to volunteer. To learn how you can help, write to info@westmarinreview.org.

Molly Marcussen, *Untitled,* 2008, mixed media collage on masonite, 7 x 7 inches